Media, Culture, and Decolonization

Media, Culture, and Decolonization

....

Re-righting the Subaltern Histories of Ghana

WUNPINI FATIMATA MOHAMMED

Rutgers University Press

New Brunswick, Camden, and Newark, New Jersey

London and Oxford

Rutgers University Press is a department of Rutgers, The State University of New Jersey, one of the leading public research universities in the nation. By publishing worldwide, it furthers the University's mission of dedication to excellence in teaching, scholarship, research, and clinical care.

Library of Congress Cataloging-in-Publication Data
Names: Mohammed, Wunpini Fatimata, author.
Title: Media, culture, and decolonization : re-righting the subaltern
    histories of Ghana / Wunpini Fatimata Mohammed.
Description: New Brunswick : Rutgers University Press, 2025. |
    Includes bibliographical references and index.
Identifiers: LCCN 2025012746 | ISBN 9781978841642 (paperback) |
    ISBN 9781978841659 (hardcover)
Subjects: LCSH: Mass media and language—Political aspects—Ghana. |
    Mass media and culture—Ghana. | Decolonization—Social aspects—Ghana. |
    Ghana—Languages. | BISAC: SOCIAL SCIENCE / Ethnic Studies /
    African Studies | POLITICAL SCIENCE / World / African
Classification: LCC P96.L342 G43 2025 | DDC 302.2309667—dc23/eng/20250326
LC record available at https://lccn.loc.gov/2025012746

A British Cataloging-in-Publication record for this book is available from the British Library.

Partial funding provided by the Hull Memorial Publication Fund of Cornell University.

References to internet websites (URLs) were accurate at the time of writing. Neither the author nor Rutgers University Press is responsible for URLs that may have expired or changed since the manuscript was prepared.

♾ The paper used in this publication meets the requirements of the American National Standard for Information Sciences—Permanence of Paper for Printed Library Materials, ANSI Z39.48-1992.

rutgersuniversitypress.org

For all bilchininima

Kundi Yelkpana

Lahabaya-soparisi, Ta-aada ni Maŋsulinsi: Gana Tarimba Taarihinim mali zali, nyela kundi shɛli din tiri ti maŋsulinsi ninkpali zaŋ kpa ti lahabaya-soparisi ni ti taɣaada nim polo. Kundi ŋɔ nyɛla din kpuɣi gbaŋsabila bala yɛltɔɣa, ni bi kaya ni taɣaada n zaŋ zahim lahabaya-soparisi din be Dagbaŋ baŋsim ni milinsi dundɔŋ ni. Di nyɛla pini karili n zaŋ ti niri kam ŋun mali taɣaada, bala yɛltɔɣa, ni lahabaya-soparisi baŋsima korisi. Kundi maa zaŋ la di nini n kpa Gana tingbani ni, gbaŋsabila yɛltɔɣa soparisi din gbaai shini, lahaba'churi/talivisa, ni walansi; n naan yi kpaŋsi maŋsulinsi yɛmbahinga, ni di zaŋ tum tuma tiŋbihi baŋsim sodolisi laɣim'gbaai ni. Di porimi gbaai duniya zaa tingbana din salo galisi moya, n naan yi kahagiri so shɛŋa dabsimbandi ni tingbana-dunba-taba ni mali n labisiri maŋsulinsi nyaanga. Di wurindi la tingbaŋ puuni tarinli ni gaŋbu-gaŋbu, n kahagiri di dangana ni niɣima balbu din be taɣaada nim kpiribu ni. Kundi ŋɔ buɣisiri la yiko shɛli gbaŋsabila yɛltɔɣa soparisi ni mali ni di tooi kpaŋsi maŋsulinsi din be taɣaada ni milinsi puuni.

About This Book

Media, Culture, and Decolonization: Re-righting the Subaltern Histories of Ghana invites us to look at media and culture from a decolonial perspective. Through Dagbaŋ epistemologies and knowledge systems, this book examines media by highlighting how African languages, cultures, and traditions can shift how we think of knowledge. It is an offering to anyone curious about the relationship between culture, language and media. By focusing on African-language media in Ghana such as film, television, and radio, the book emphasizes the importance of espousing a decolonial politic and praxis in the process of cocreating knowledge with Indigenous communities. It connects the struggles of Global Majority countries and demonstrates the ways in which (neo) colonialism and imperialism impede the work toward liberatory futures. This book demonstrates the potential that African-language media hold as tools of cultural and epistemological decolonization.

Contents

Media, Culture, and Decolonization

Introduction

● ●

Decolonizing African
Media Studies

Sɔli din viɛla ni laɣim so'chandiba

I was born and raised in Tamale, Ghana. I spent most of my childhood in what is today one of Ghana's largest cities and is currently leading a cultural revolution in the country. For most of my life, Northern Ghana was framed and treated as merely a spectator in Ghanaian cultural production, discussions around nationalism, and even celebrations of Ghanaian history. I had a sense of this growing up in Zogbeli, Tamale, through my consumption of television and radio content, which was largely shaped by my parents' ideological and political interests. In the 1990s, the Ghanaian media landscape had not been fully liberalized, so I witnessed the ways in which censorship shaped and regulated media content on television and radio. From hearing about strategies that my uncle employed to resist President J. J. Rawlings's state propaganda to being limited to one television channel, Ghana Television (GTV), for all our entertainment needs, I began to learn unconsciously about the ways in which Ghana's political and economic landscape shaped media production, distribution and consumption.

When I returned home from school in the afternoon I often watched with my brother the Cartoon Network on GTV, which regaled us with tales from *Dexter's Laboratory, The Power Puff Girls, Johnny Bravo,* and *Tom & Jerry,* among others. Saturday mornings were special as we woke up early to take a bath and watch the Cartoon Network. Late morning, I would walk with my

1

brother and a neighborhood friend to the regional library in the central business district of Tamale to embark on the series of adventures that books including those in the Babysitters Club Series, the Pacesetters, Mactracks, the African Writers Series, and Heinemann had to offer. We would read for a few hours, break for lunch, and then return to wrap up reading and select the books that we would borrow to take home. We were so caught up in our love for adventure that if we heard that a kid had access to any Disney films, we would arrange to visit their home to join in the viewing. We read books at the regional library and sought out films to match our imaginations to what the producers and directors had actualized on screen. It wasn't until I was in graduate school in the United States, when I began to think more critically about concepts like globalization, Anglo-American dominance, cultural hybridity, and cultural imperialism, that I began to reflect more critically on my childhood experiences with media.

As a child, I knew that the people I saw on GTV often did not speak my language. I could engage English content like the Ghanaian films of the time, but I felt that there was something missing when it came to Indigenous-language content, specifically in my first language, Dagbanli. Akan-language content often dominated entertainment media, and English-language content dominated the news and current affairs programs, including coverage of state events such as Independence Day, May Day, and others. The Akan language, Twi, is the dominant tongue of Southern Ghana. For a time, *Showcase in Dagbani*, which would air occasionally, was the highlight of our days. This program presented an opportunity for many people in the Northern Region who did not speak English or the dominant Akan languages to feel represented on TV. For many others who did not speak English or Dagbanli and were from marginalized Northern ethnic groups whose languages were not taught and examined in schools, they never saw themselves represented at all.

As I watched talk show hosts on what many of us children considered boring programs such as *Talking Point* and *The Breakfast Show* on GTV, I noticed that I barely saw my identities as a Dagbana, a Muslim, and a woman represented. And often, if some of these hosts and TV presenters were women and/or occasionally Muslim, they were rarely ever from any ethnic group of the North. Seeing myself represented in these ways was important to me because I was raised in a household in which my parents made sure that I was connected to my culture and history. While children of other "educated" members of my community were shielded from direct engagement with and immersion into their culture, my parents pulled us more into our ancestral cultures and histories. For example, I grew up feeling different because I often found myself playing with children who had only Muslim names. I often cursed my parents for giving me a Dagbanli name, Wunpini, which amplified my difference from children who I believed had cool names like Ayisha, Mariam, Sadia. My father was proud of his Dagbaŋ heritage and made sure that even though we had Muslim middle names, our Dagbanli first names were what everyone knew and called us by. Now when I reflect on it, I am thankful because while some of my age mates are beginning to go back to adopt Dagbanli names for themselves and go through hoops to have them reflected in their official documents, I do not have to hassle with that. We also often spent our school holidays with our family in Yendi and Zabzugu, where we not only learned different variations of Dagbanli but also were immersed in our ethnic culture and values. We spent time with grandparents, aunties, uncles, and cousins who strengthened our connections to our culture. In fact, my first experiences of engaging with Dagbaŋ folktales through storytelling were in Yendi, where we would spend nights listening to stories about the cunning ways of the Kpatinariga (spider), widely known in Southern Ghana as Ananse the spider. It wasn't until I was seventeen and accepted to college that I visited the nation's capital Accra for the first time. Therefore, although I was largely shielded from engaging American or British media products that were more widely available in Accra on private commercial media organizations, I still got a taste of it through books and some of the programming on GTV that was broadcast nationwide.

During my childhood, there was a weekly Sunday musical drama on GTV called *Cantata* that explored a range of social issues such as marriage and family. This program was in the Akan languages, and I usually had to rely on my mother to watch with me and translate. When the trend of holding marriage ceremonies on Sundays began to pick up in Tamale in the late 1990s, I lost a translator since my mother had to be at one event or another, leaving me to watch *Cantata* with very little understanding since subtitles were not offered for the show. I realized then that beyond English-language content, there was very little commitment to representing my ethnic identity and other Northern ethnic identities on national television. This erasure is particularly interesting to note because after Akan, the Mole-Dagbanli language group has the largest number of speakers, but we are rarely represented in advertisements, TV shows, telecom company helplines, or other narratives on TV stations with nationwide coverage. Instead, various efforts at Indigenous-language media representation focus on Akan, Ga, Ewe, and sometimes Fante, all languages of Southern Ghana. Occasionally, Hausa is used to "represent" Ghana's North even though the largest number of Hausa speakers are concentrated in the greater Accra and Ashanti regions (in the South). Again, despite its sizeable population, the North continues to be symbolically annihilated in media representations even today. Since the 2010s, there has been a growth in satellite TV channels in the Northern Region's capital Tamale, like Sagani TV, NTV, and more recently Zaa TV, which provide programming in Dagbanli. Again, people who have no access to satellite TV and still depend on terrestrial transmissions are often excluded from engaging with this type of content. Radio therefore continues to be the most accessible media platform for people in Northern Ghana and across the nation and the continent.

Therefore, I come to this project as a Northern Ghanaian, Dagbana and woman who grew up watching movies, reading newspapers, and listening ardently to radio programs. I draw from my experiences as a radio journalist in Tamale and Accra to enrich the analysis. My analysis of the film and TV industries is shaped by my observations of the industries and perspectives as a young audience member. The extent of my industry experience is limited to the radio and digital media industries. Throughout the book, I use the terms Dagbamba, Dagbanli, and Dagbaŋ as opposed to Dagomba, Dagbani, and Dagbon to reflect how the communities refer to themselves rather than colonial corruptions or elite constructions of the naming of this community. Thus, Dagbamba are the people/ethnicity (singular Dagbana), Dagbanli is the language, and Dagbaŋ is the community/kingdom. Resistance to these corruptive referents that have been mainstreamed is my own way of reflecting the identities and experiences of the Dagbaŋ masses back to them while re-righting our histories and narratives.

Ultimately, these inequalities in media accessibility and representation piqued my interest in media and the power that media held to affirm, marginalize, and erase certain identities. I say all of this to provide background on how I came to be interested in Indigenous-language media and indigeneity in Ghana and elsewhere. I share these experiences to provide a larger context for the development of Indigenous-language media in Northern Ghana through film, radio, and television and to highlight the role they played in these communities as a tool of culture making, cultural affirmation, and cultural preservation/documentation. I argue here that to understand the marginalization of African media studies, it is imperative to examine the most marginalized media histories and political economies within the national context, using Ghana as an example. In this book, therefore, I re-right history by bringing attention to the Ghanaian media histories that have been perpetually erased due to a range of structural factors. I will discuss this further in later chapters.

Media Studies in Africa

African media studies is a discipline that has historically been marginalized in the global academy (Asante, 2019; Gadzekpo, 2009). This marginalization means that much of the research and knowledge production on African media studies is dominated by white northern scholars, many of whom self-identify as Africanists (Chigudu, 2019; Jeater, 2018). Among other things the marginalization of Africans in the field of media studies can be attributed to a host of factors, some of which include limited access to funding opportunities, limited opportunities for professional development, a lack of mentorship for students and early career scholars, expensive tuition for graduate education on the continent and elsewhere, and institutional and systemic barriers to professional development in the areas of academic publishing, conference participation, public scholarship, and job opportunities and security.

Conversations that have examined the overwhelmingly white nature of the field of communication(s) and media studies (Shome, 2000) have often left out African media studies focusing instead on the way that the discipline has marginalized scholars in the Black/African diaspora and Asian, Middle Eastern, and Latine scholars. Asante (2019) succinctly notes that that the "mere 'inclusion' and 'tolerance' of difference with regard to race, class, gender, ability, sexuality and nationality cannot address the violence of White capitalist heteropatriarchy in academia" (p. 485). Very often there is little mention of scholarship on Indigenous media studies in North America, Australia, and New Zealand. This marginalization is evident in the lack of representation of African media scholars and scholarship in major communication conferences such as the "global" International Communication Association and the National Communication Association (USA). There is no division or interest group at either of these conferences specifically dedicated to African media, rhetoric and communication studies, and the little representation of African scholarship at these conferences is from white scholars and a handful of Global North-based Indigenous African scholars like myself.

While conversations like #CommunicationSoWhite have shaken up the status quo in the field over the past few years and have highlighted the ways in which racism, white supremacy, colonization, slavery, and imperialism color the epistemological values and the content of knowledge production in the field (Chakravartty et al., 2018; Ng et al., 2020), African media studies as usual gets glossed over or not mentioned at all in these efforts at decolonizing the discipline. And when it is discussed, there is a disproportionate focus on South Africa, which has historically been the default country to represent all of "Africa."

Here, I highlight the marginalization of African media studies in the larger discipline of global media studies drawing on my experiences as an African student and early career scholar based in the Global North academy. To understand the importance of this book to African and global discussions around media studies, we need to pay attention to the way that African scholarship is treated in the global academy.

In the introduction and in chapter 1, I employ an African feminist autoethnography to explore the tools that decolonization and Indigenous African knowledge systems present us with in our efforts to disrupt this racist, heteropatriarchal, white supremacist status quo. Using Northern Ghana as a focus, I examine the challenges mitigating the growth of African media studies, drawing extensively on my experiences as a Ghanaian-born scholar who migrated to the United States to study and later work in the academy. Although this book is grounded in my experiences and scholarship as an African media studies scholar, the observations made and the interventions presented can be extrapolated to understand the marginalization of Africans and African perspectives in broader, related fields. Therefore, to understand the challenges mitigating the growth of African media scholarship produced by Africans, it is imperative to understand the lived experience of Africans in the academy and pay attention to how our experiences can guide the field toward a path of decolonization.

Africa, Decolonization, and Media Studies

For a long time, African stories have been told by white scholars in the academy, many of whom know too little of the contexts of these communities to bring the narratives the nuance they deserve. Misrepresentation of African communities in research is as rife as the misrepresentation of Indigenous communities in North America, Australia, and New Zealand in scholarship (Smith, 2012). The danger of this phenomenon is that written knowledge mostly produced in ivory towers, presented in inaccessible language, and published in paywalled journals inaccessible to the masses has come to be regarded by default as the truth of these communities while Indigenous ways of knowing that have been sustained for centuries by Indigenous communities are pushed to the periphery of knowledge production and are rarely recognized as legitimate systems of knowing (Mignolo and Walsh, 2018; Mohammed, 2019; Smith, 2012; wa Thiong'o 1986). According to Ndlovu-Gatsheni (2013, p. 8), "Since the time of the European Renaissance and Enlightenment, Westerners worked tirelessly to make their knowledge the only truthful and universal knowledge and ceaselessly spread it through Christianity and other means across the world, in the process appropriating and displacing existing African knowledges. Western knowledge and imperial power worked together to inscribe coloniality across the African continent and other parts of the non-Western world." In the field of media studies, this phenomenon faces a double bind in the analysis of media representations and the study of how media is situated in the cultural, social, political, religious, and economic mold of these communities. This power imbalance that advantages foreign (usually white) scholars' access to African scholarship and scholarly production means that in many cases the single story is what becomes the dominant narrative. Scholars like Omotayo Banjo (2019), in her edited book *Media Across the African Diaspora: Content, Audiences, and Global Influence*, work to address the single-story narrative. Banjo sought to "celebrate the contributions of people of African descent around the world, as well as to capture some of the struggles that people of African descent continue to face in their endeavors to tell stories which reflect their multifaceted experiences and narratives" (2019, p. 1). Similarly, Clark and Mohammed (2023) in their *African Women in Digital Spaces: Redefining Social Movements on the Continent and in the Diaspora* present perspectives on the way that African women and feminists use digital media platforms to build liberatory futures.

Various African scholars in media and communication(s) study the continent and its diaspora from various perspectives. It is imperative to note, however, that very few African scholars in the field theorize from within the continent, and even fewer ground their work in Indigenous African epistemologies. Although scholars of African media studies and communication studies have theorized extensively in the field and brought invaluable insights that have shaped the growth of the field, African media studies is still dominated by white scholars. A cursory look at the scholarly output in African studies shows that white voices dominate the construction of the narratives around the situatedness of media in African communities (Chigudu, 2019; Shome, 2000; Sobande, 2018). Therefore, the project of decolonization and employing antiracist, anti-imperialist approaches to knowledge production on the continent is long overdue.

There is a little hope however in work by a few white scholars on decolonizing media studies and decentering white, Global North ways of knowing that have historically been used to erase work by Indigenous scholars around the world. Shohat and Stam's (1994) *Unthinking Eurocentrism: Multiculturalism and the Media* invites us to reexamine everything that we have been taught and everything that we know about media studies in the Global South that not only are racist but have reinscribed Global North values and specifically Anglo-American dominance and white supremacy. Whereas it is imperative to move from a reactionary stance on the marginalization of our African systems of knowing, it is important to understand how our communities are situated in global geopolitics and the way that global power dynamics further push us to the periphery of knowledge production. It is therefore important to acknowledge that ". . . Eurocentrism sanitizes Western history while patronizing and even demonizing the non-West; it thinks of itself in terms of its noblest achievements—science, progress, humanism—but of the non-West in terms of deficiencies, real or imagined" (Shohat and Stam, 1994, p. 3). This way, as we produce knowledge on media about our communities, we keep in mind the way that power politics have actively frustrated and undercut our efforts at producing knowledge in the academy for Africans by Africans. This book unthinks eurocentrism by theorizing media in marginalized communities through a groundedness in indigeneity.

Unthinking eurocentrism not only calls for a dismantling of the Western canon but also prompts us to decenter knowledge production from the Global North and work from the peripheries where our knowledge systems have been pushed. Decentering the Western canon is strongly connected to the process of decolonization, "the process of revealing and dismantling colonialist power in all its forms" (Ashcroft et al., 2000, p. 63). Decolonization cannot happen in a vacuum, so cannot be divorced from the roots of slavery, colonialism, and imperialism that have produced the need for its existence. To truly understand decolonization, we need to situate it "in relation to globalization and new imperialist formations" (Loomba, 2005, p. 1) so that we can work toward dismantling these oppressive structures in our societies.

The process of decolonization is entangled not only in undoing oppressive systems and structures but also in ensuring that this process of undoing significantly improves the lived reality of victims of colonization globally. Decolonization of knowledge production in the academy is needed now more than ever because academia has historically been and is currently implicated in colonialism and neocolonialism. For example, disciplines like anthropology were built on the field's complicity with colonizers, providing them with tools to better colonize Indigenous peoples (Roque, 2003).

As we explore ways of decolonizing African media studies, it is imperative for us to amplify and highlight the ways in which some media studies scholars have worked to expand the field to center African systems of knowing (Isika and Assay, 2008; Mohammed, 2022a; Mohammed, 2019; Moyo, 2020; Ugboajah, 1985), opening us up to the potential of looking beyond the West and to our own communities for answers that plague us in our processes of knowledge production. While transdisciplinarity is important for this project, we must theorize from the margins and look to other Global South contexts to make connections to our lived experiences and how these connections can enable us to produce collaborative projects that facilitate the process of decolonization.

In chapter 1, I demonstrate the ways in which South-South relationships can guide us toward decolonizing knowledge production. Smith (2012), in *Decolonizing Methodologies: Research and Indigenous Peoples*, demonstrates the possibilities of mapping and connecting the condition of Global South Indigenous communities for producing decolonial knowledge. Ngũgĩ wa Thiong'o (1986) has also shown us that our Indigenous languages, literatures, and knowledge systems hold immense potential in facilitating the decolonization of African studies. This is the work that I build on to deconstruct the relationship between Indigenous-language media and Indigenous epistemologies in Ghana.

Indigenous Knowledge Systems in African Media Studies

While media studies is considered a relatively new discipline compared to other disciplines, there has not been enough knowledge produced in the field by Africans about Africa. Continentally, there has been extensive focus on practical training in the areas of journalism, film, new media, and so forth (Fosu, 2011). While it is important to work toward the practical training of media makers and content creators, it is imperative to examine not only how theory can be used to shape the training of media practitioners but also how it can be used to build a body of knowledge to support the growth of the discipline on the continent. Like many other disciplines, this field suffers a paucity of resources to support epistemological growth on the continent (Gadzekpo, 2009).

In my journey to contribute to knowledge in African media studies, I have stumbled through a myriad of challenges, some of which include barriers enforced by mostly white gatekeepers of the academy. According to Chakravartty et al. (2018), "Non-White scholars continue to be underrepresented in publication rates, citation rates, and editorial positions in communication studies" (p. 254). The situation is even more dire in the field of African media studies, which is dominated by white scholars. Most African academic journals were founded in the 2000s, with a third of them based in South Africa (Murray, 2014). Ultimately, there are not enough academic journals focused on Africa that are also based in Africa, therefore African media scholars are compelled to expand the scope of the platforms where they publish their work to include international journals, which are usually based in the Global North. Early-career scholars of Africa based in the Global North who attempt to place their work in African journals to reach African audiences are often discouraged because Northern institutions generally question the legitimacy and rigor of African journals, a phenomenon that is a direct product of imperialism and white supremacy. Africans studying media are specifically presented with barriers by (white) Global North gatekeepers who question their legitimacy to study their own communities and their "objectivity," epistemological rigor, and many others. While some of these critiques of scholarship by Africans may be valid and help improve their research, many of them are grounded in white supremacy and racist assumptions. Other people of color in the Global North and South have faced similar challenges, where in some cases their linguistic proficiency in English is used to measure their intelligence and competence as scholars of fields that they have studied for years.

Although African media scholars like Ugboajah (1985), Isika and Assay (2008), and Moyo (2020) have theorized drawing on African cultures and knowledge systems to produce epistemology to understand media studies on the continent, much work needs to be done to not only decolonize African media studies but also center Indigenous ways of knowing and explore the potential they hold for the growth of African media studies. This book does exactly that by repositioning African media and scholarship as a site for radical politics. The absence of African media scholarship in graduate classes meant that as a graduate student and an early career scholar I had to curate my graduate education and scholarship to address my epistemological needs. In a decolonized classroom, the burden should not be on students to single-handedly nurture their own professional and academic growth.

On this journey of curating my own education, I learned the value of trans-disciplinarity/interdisciplinarity. Having been trained in a transdisciplinary background since my undergraduate study, I took advantage of my familiarity with working in transdisciplinary spaces to allow myself to explore what these spaces hold for African media studies scholarship and research. It was while working on some of my earlier projects in which I could not find any legacy, "canonical" theories and conceptual frameworks to understand the phenomenon I was studying that I started reading beyond media studies. I explored scholarship in literary and language studies and ultimately found my way home to the wealth of knowledge that is in African Indigenous knowledge systems. These epistemological forays showed me the importance of not only thinking beyond geographical constraints but also examining how the colonial condition produced shared realities in communities across the Global South. Ngũgĩ wa Thiong'o (1986) and Linda Tuhiwai Smith (2012) show us the beauty and potential of imagining sites of knowledge production beyond the northern academy. Smith's (2012) acknowledgment of the parallels between her work and Ngũgĩ's drew me closer to further exploring Indigenous knowledge systems in Africa and to unpack their potential for theorizing media in this book. Here, Smith and wa Thiong'o give us the tools to understand how important it is to disrupt canonical thinking. While the process of epistemic decolonization must be global, it is imperative to note the globality of coloniality while acknowledging the peculiarities of colonial conditions in various continental contexts (Mignolo and Walsh, 2018).

In the conceptualization of Indigenous knowledge systems and the invaluable potential they hold to facilitate the growth of decolonial research in the Global South, they teach us not only how to conduct ethical research in Indigenous communities but also the importance of centering the most marginalized communities in our scholarship. Conceptualizing Indigenous African knowledge systems to study media in West Africa has opened me to a whole new area of study that was not only linguistically marginalized but also epistemologically marginalized.

Indigenous African knowledge systems give us the tools to think freely and break out of the mold that the Northern canon constricts us in. Our African knowledge systems also equip us with the tools to think creatively and customize extant "canonical" theories to apply to our specific national, economic, political, religious, and sociocultural contexts. Where these canons fall short, we open ourselves to breaking the mold and creating language, coining phrases and concepts to better understand the phenomena we are studying. Theorizing from the margins and disrupting the canon do not come without challenges. I expound on these epistemological innovations in chapter 1.

When exploring ways to theorize from the margins and centering knowledge systems in Global South communities, we are constantly undercut by the racist, colonial, white supremacist, capitalist heteropatriarchy within which we are operating. Decolonizing African media studies also means opening ourselves to epistemological flexibility where we look to other Global South contexts that we share cultural proximity with to draw on theories, concepts, and methods to study our own communities. I demonstrate the importance of these South-South epistemological forays and connections throughout the book.

Indigenous-Language Media

In the beginning of this introduction, I shared my personal experiences and used them to foreground the need for decolonizing scholarship and centering marginalized communities in Ghanaian media production. Here, I discuss the state of Indigenous-language media in the country today. Although Indigenous-language media is often popular with the majority of the Ghanaian populace, there is very little investment in research and production around this type of media. In the area of film, industries such as the Dagbanli film industry get no governmental support to develop content for their audiences. In the radio sector, however, tremendous strides have been made across the country to bring content such as news and talk shows, educational programs, and others to rural and urban audiences in languages like Twi, Ga, Ewe, Waale, Gonja, and Dagbanli. More recently on satellite television, there has been an extensive development of programming to address the various cultural and linguistic needs of people who speak Ghanaian languages, although there is still room for improvement regarding content and the diversity of languages represented on TV. In this book, I discuss the relationships between various media platforms like television, radio, and film to demonstrate the centrality of Ghanaian languages to the country's mediascape. Our efforts to decolonize African media become incomplete when we fail to pay attention to and theorize about the relationships between culture, language, and media.

In decolonizing African media studies, we need to concern ourselves with the ways in which certain types of media and systems of knowing are deemed illegitimate by gatekeepers of the field. For example, although Indigenous-language media in Africa constitutes a significant proportion of media content in West Africa, specifically in Ghana it is grossly undertheorized for a myriad of reasons (Mohammed, 2019; Salawu, 2011). Many scholars who dominate the field are non-Africans who are not competent enough in Indigenous languages to undertake projects of knowledge production that center these systems. The few existing African scholars who are intellectually and linguistically equipped to undertake this type of research do not have access to the funds and resources that would enable them to actualize these projects. This paucity of knowledge on Indigenous-language media content means that we are constantly supporting and reinscribing the Western canon. This book therefore foregrounds marginalized ways of knowing while highlighting the ways in which Indigenous communities are disrupting, challenging, and resisting the canon epistemologically, axiologically, and ontologically.

With recent continental, diasporic, and global interests in African media (by way of YouTube, Amazon Prime Video, Netflix Naija, Netflix MENA, and Netflix South Africa), African media studies is strategically positioned to provide critical and nuanced analyses on media content and to gently nudge content creators toward producing media that not only affirms Africanness in its myriad of iterations but also produces content that awakens the consciousness of Africans and our siblings in the diaspora who were taken from us.

Research Sites and Methods

To understand the political economy of media industries in Northern Ghana, it is imperative to understand the sites of research and the backgrounds of the interlocutors of this book project. In this section, I discuss the methods that produced the main arguments of the book. Here, I demonstrate the importance of contextualizing tools of inquiry to suit the sociocultural context of the communities studied. While here I provide an overview, I delve deeper into the methodological and theoretical underpinning of the book in chapter 1. Due to the complex nature of the topic, a hybrid approach was employed to unpack the intricacies of the political economy of media in Northern Ghana. I employed qualitative methods such as archival research, participant observation, in-depth interviews, and communal conversation circles (CCCs), defined extensively in chapter 1. Interviews and participant observation were conducted in Tamale, and CCCs were held in three rural communities near Tamale. By utilizing these methods, I covered film production, distribution, and audience reception. Most of the data for this study were collected in the rainy season of 2018, with follow-up data gathered in 2023. The research sites were urban and rural communities in the Northern Region.

I began data collection by engaging in participant observation on the field. After becoming familiar with the research site, I interviewed key stakeholders such as filmmakers and distributors. I conducted CCCs among film audiences to understand how they interact with, consume, and read Dagbanli films. I conducted a total of seventeen interviews and seven CCCs. Altogether, eleven industry pioneers were interviewed. Four of the interviews were conducted in English, seven in Dagbanli. All six interviews with distributors and seven CCCs were conducted in Dagbanli. Interviews with pioneering filmmakers lasted an average of one hour. Interviews with distributors averaged thirty minutes, and CCCs ran for an average of forty minutes.

I interviewed eleven pioneering filmmakers, two of whom were part of the production of the first Dagbanli film released in 1989. Later in the book, I demonstrate how the referent "filmmaker" is disrupted by the organic and needful blurring of lines between the work of directors and actors in film production. Of the eleven filmmakers, only one was a woman. These filmmakers were present and contributed to key turning points in the history of film in the Northern Region. Most of these filmmakers had a minimum of ten years of filmmaking experience. My professional relationship with the then-president of the Northern Drama and Filmmakers Association (NORDRAFIM), Alhassan Yushawu Jahanfo, facilitated my access to these industry pioneers. I collaborated with Jahanfo to sample the various interlocutors for this study. We worked together to sample the filmmakers with the most industry experience, paying attention to purposively select active filmmakers who were present at and participated in the birth of the film industry. Together with Jahanfo, I sampled filmmakers who were involved in the birth and evolution of the film industry and who still worked in the industry or mentored upcoming filmmakers. All key members whose perspectives were important to the narrative were interviewed. In cases where filmmakers were not available for interviews (e.g., Zakaria Abdullai, popularly known as Zakvilla) because they had passed away, their family and mentees who worked closely with them and who were still active in the industry were interviewed.

With the guidance of NORDRAFIM, I selected five distribution centers to observe over five weeks. All the distribution centers were located in the central business district of Tamale. They were selected based on which centers were most popular with film distribution, which recorded the highest sales, and were widely known by vendors who bought films for retail in villages across the Northern Region. These centers also had connections with distributors in Accra and Kumasi to whom they sent DVDs for distribution. After several conversations with the president of NORDRAFIM, I decided to observe the key distribution shops that sold the most DVDs. I interviewed six distributors to learn more about the business side and geographical reach of distribution and the power politics in film distribution in the industry. I interviewed six distributors but observed five distribution centers because one of the distributors interviewed owned a mobile vehicle with which he moved from place to place to distribute films. I did not conduct observation with this distributor. He was, however, included in the sample because he was one of the early mobile distributors of films in the region. Of the six distributors sampled, three were women. One of the six distributors was a mobile distributor who drove from village to village to sell CDs, and the remaining five operated or supervised operations at distribution shops in Tamale. For five weeks, I observed five distribution shops.

I observed five NORDRAFIM meetings over five weeks. Each meeting lasted for two hours and had about forty to fifty people in attendance, with the majority men. There was an average of ten women attendees at meetings. Most of the interlocutors here were youthful actors and directors, some of whom were representing their drama groups at the meetings. A few pioneering filmmakers would attend or send representatives from their drama groups. I participated in a NORDRAFIM-supported film workshop over a period of two days as part of the Ghana International Film Week celebrations. In attendance were filmmakers, distributors, actors, and producers. Most pioneering filmmakers were present throughout most of the programs, and actors based outside Tamale traveled to the city each day for the program. Like most programs, only one woman pioneering filmmaker sat at the high table with the other pioneers.

After eight weeks of interviews with filmmakers and distributors and observing distribution shops and NORDRAFIM weekly meetings, I conducted CCCs in the villages where movies were usually filmed. These villages were selected because they constituted the most active viewing population due to their proximity to filmmakers and film production. These villages were usually mentioned by filmmakers interviewed as the ideal locations for filming and as the most active viewership population. I conducted seven CCCs in Napaɣayili (two), Kpilo (three), and Yɔŋ Dakpemyili (two). All three villages are Dagbanli-speaking communities in the Northern Region. CCCs were organized based on gender; interlocutors usually consisted of an all-male or all-female group. There were three CCCs consisting of women and four consisting of men. At least one all-male and one all-female CCC was conducted in each village sampled. Although I had set out to conduct three all-male and three all-female CCCs, my handler who helped organize the CCCs accidentally put together two all-male CCCs in one of the villages. I initially wanted to dissolve the third CCC, but he advised that the interlocutors would not be happy and might not provide further access. Therefore, I proceeded to have a conversation with the members of the group and included them in the sample. On average, there were six to eight interlocutors in each CCC.

I arrived in the field in 2018 during Ramadan, a month on the Islamic calendar when Muslims observe fasting and holiness as required by Islam. Ramadan is one of the five pillars of Islam that Muslims are entreated to participate in and hold in high regard. I followed conventions by putting interviews and CCCs on hold until after the Ramadan. Most entertainment activities come to a halt during Ramadan, so most filmmakers took a break from filming to observe the holy month. I made the decision to wait until after Ramadan to conduct interviews and CCCs because interlocutors would generally refrain from discussing contentious issues in observance of the holy month. I also learned during interviews with filmmakers that because most actors who are Muslim refrain from eating, their lack of energy may impede their ability to do their work well, so it was ideal to put filmmaking on hold during this time.

However, a few Muslim filmmakers, like Yakubu Saani (Lawyer Gbaɣinli), who worked in the comedy genre, continued filming during this period. This period also overlapped with the season when farmers went away to work on farms. According to distributors, sales were usually low during the farming season and went up during harvest season because then farmers had sold their farm produce and could afford to purchase films. Therefore, I spent the last few weeks of Ramadan (and peak farming season) to observe the activities of distribution centers. I spent this period observing distribution shops in Tamale to study sales during this period. The interviews, CCCs, and participant observation covered various topics such as peak sales periods, the evolution of sales since the inception of the film industry, and the dynamics of wholesale and retail, among others. During data collection, topics on the history of the film industry (from its inception to the present), film production, distribution, and reception were extensively covered.

In January 2023, I returned to Tamale to gather follow-up data to support the argument of this book. I spent seven months consuming satellite television and interviewing stakeholders in the satellite television industry such as presenters, program managers, and TV station managers. I also spent time watching TV programs such as *Kavini* on Sagani TV and *Baŋsim Chuɣu* on Zaa TV to learn more about the cultures and traditions of Dagbamba. In addition, I interviewed stakeholders such as *lunsi* to learn more about their work. In total, I interviewed five stakeholders in the television industry, one griot (luŋa), and the director of literacy at the Ghana Institute of Linguistics, Literacy and Bible Translation. I used these follow-up data to expand on and strengthen my argument on the silenced histories of media in Ghana.

Outline of the Book

The book focuses on the Northern Region of Ghana but puts the political economy of Northern Ghanaian media into the larger context of Ghanaian media histories and their relationship with global media. I open the book by putting it in conversation with the timely topic of decolonization that shapes the theoretical underpinning of the book and serves as the backdrop against which the arguments of the book are made. By opening the book with discussions on decolonization, I journey with readers to reflect on power, colonization, and imperialism and the ways in which they shape media industries in the Global South. I also provide a reflection on the politics of knowledge production and my situatedness as a Northern Ghanaian woman in regional, national, and global politics on knowledge making. This book maps the histories of marginalized media industries in Ghana. Here, I am not concerned with solely analyzing Dagbanli movies or programming on radio or satellite TV; I focus rather on understanding the ways in which culture, politics, and tradition shape the media ecologies of these industries. Where necessary, I bring attention to how TV and film content is grounded in Indigenous knowledges and how these platforms serve as sites of resistance and cultural affirmation for audience communities in this region.

In chapter 1, I delve deeper into the politics of epistemology and how that has historically been shaped by structural factors. I provide a critical reflection on the community-influenced methodological innovations I made and how that enabled me to engage communities ethically and respectfully. I bring attention to the undertheorized area of indigeneity in Africa and for that matter Ghana and deconstruct my experiences as a researcher and community member and how that shaped my engagement with the community. By reflecting on Indigenous epistemologies in Ghana and connecting them to other parts of Africa and the world, I highlight not only the potential of South-South connections to resist and challenge the Western canon but also their potential to open us up to new ways of thinking about knowledge making and how they relate to ontology and axiology. In chapter 2 I map the history of technology, literacy, and media in Northern Ghana to demonstrate how politics combines with structural factors to shape media histories in the region. Here, we learn about media convergence and are guided by history to understand the relationships between radio, TV and film.

In chapter 3, I deconstruct subalternity by drawing connections between Indigenous ways of knowing via folklore and griot culture and what is known as contemporary media such as film, radio and television. I foreground the work of the griots/lunsi demonstrating how they contribute to culture-making, knowledge production and history transmission. I argue that while efforts have been made by scholars to distinguish between traditional media and art forms such as folklore, folk songs, historical narratives, and contemporary media such as popular music, film, radio, and others, these media forms blur into and shape each other. In chapter 4, I present a history of Dagbanli films, drawing attention to the ways in which social, political, religious, economic, and cultural factors have shaped the evolution of the industry.

In chapter 5 I discuss the relationship between movies, the politics of distributing movies to audiences, and the way that current affairs and the news landscape shape various thematic aspects of the films produced. Here, I present an analysis of the channels of film distribution and how that is intertwined with the urban architecture of Tamale. We learn that despite the challenges faced by film distributors, they have worked and built on innovative marketing strategies to get their products to their core audiences, especially in rural Northern Ghana.

In chapter 6 I track the history of television in the Ghanaian mediascape. Here, I draw connections between Indigenous-language television stations and the work they do to promote social change in communities. I argue that the values underpinning the operations of some of these stations parallel Ghanaian Pan-African liberation fighter Kwame Nkrumah's dream about the potential of socialist television to bring about social consciousness and transformation in the country. I then wrap up the book by pointing to future projections about subaltern media and the importance of resisting cultural imperialism.

This book is an important personal project of writing subaltern communities back into Ghanaian media and national histories, inspired by my desire to see people like me and my community represented in the histories of Ghana. That I draw on Indigenous knowledges to demonstrate the importance of the political economy of these media industries highlights why Africans should theorize about our communities using our own knowledges and philosophies. African scholars who have often found Western theories and ontologies inadequate for theorizing African realities may find inspiration from the arguments that I make throughout the book to begin theorizing from their own positions *with* their own communities.

That this book is the first of its kind that examines the Indigenous-language film, radio, and TV industries in Ghana tells us how our own ways of knowing have been marginalized in academic spaces of knowledge production. That it is also the first book that foregrounds marginalized media histories and political economies in Ghana since much of media studies scholarship on Africa focuses on English, French, Portuguese, and Arabic media tells us that there is a lot of work to be done to decolonize our minds and our scholarly work. The epistemological innovations that guided the research on the book bring attention to the importance of learning from Indigenous knowledge systems and letting them guide our work. I conclude by asserting that it is time for us, as African scholars, to look deeply into our communities for guidance on knowledge cocreation and building liberatory futures.

1

Bilchiinsi Philosophy, Media, and Global Indigenous Epistemologies

• •

Bia ŋun nuu viɛla ŋuni n samdi kpiɛm dɔri

While calls for decolonization within the fields of communication studies and media studies have highlighted the white supremacy embedded in academic spaces and academic culture, not much attention has been paid to decolonization within the context of epistemology and specifically methodology. Despite renewed interest in decolonization, calls for de-Westernizing media studies can be traced to the early 2000s when James Curran and Myung-Jin Park challenged scholars to reexamine their approaches to theorizing and creating knowledge, especially in research focused on Global South communities (Glück, 2018).

In the field of media studies and more broadly, dominant Northern epistemologies have tremendously shaped curricula, the processes of knowledge production, and the content of knowledge produced (Dutta and Pal, 2020; Mohammed, 2021). Decolonization of knowledge production in media studies is imperative not only because marginalized ways of knowing have been demonized by the academy but also because of its potential to shift normative attitudes and behaviors toward knowledge in various academic settings.

Scholars interested in decolonizing methodologies should pay attention to the potential that community-focused research holds for understanding media in many African communities like Ghana, where there are often very few resources to archive media content. The challenge of archiving media content is even more dire for Indigenous-language media given their positioning in the linguistic hierarchy of media studies and media practice (Mohammed, 2019). Within the context of Northern Ghana, human-focused research in the form of ethnographic observation, interviews, and focus groups holds immense potential for documenting oral narratives about the histories and contemporary phenomena surrounding media production, distribution, and consumption.

In this chapter I draw on my experiences doing qualitative people-focused research in communities in Ghana to demonstrate the importance of decolonizing methodologies in African media studies. I reflect extensively on my experiences coproducing knowledge and shed light on the methodological interventions I made to gather knowledge ethically and respectfully in these communities. I argue that although canonical theories in communication studies and media studies such as framing theory, agenda-setting theory, and film theory can be useful in theorizing African media systems, to decolonize research we must first look to Indigenous African epistemologies and knowledge systems to support knowledge production in media studies and communication studies.

Grounding this scholarship in Northern Ghana, I discuss the potential of extrapolating my findings to understand other culturally proximal African and Global South contexts. Although my reflections focus on one community in Ghana, some epistemological nuances noted in this community may not necessarily apply to other Ghanaian, continental, or Global South communities. Where there are overlaps, I discuss and complicate them by providing contextual reflections. Here, I explicate African feminist autoethnography as a framework while presenting the methodological interventions I made when I gathered knowledge on media practices in Ghana for this book project. I also unpack Bilchiinsi as a radical philosophy for decolonizing methodologies. In the next section, I provide a larger context for conversations around decolonization and knowledge production.

Language, Knowledge Production, and Media Studies

Although conversations around decolonization in the academy have been happening for decades with scholars such as Edward Said, Frantz Fanon, Édouard Glissant, Aimé Césaire, Ngũgĩ wa Thiong'o, Ania Loomba, Walter Mignolo, Sabelo J. Ndlovu-Gatsheni, Sylvia Tamale, and Linda Tuhiwai Smith leading the way, the concept has seen renewed discussion. These conversations seem to have expanded beyond specific disciplines and have seen renewed vibrance in broader fields such as African studies (Ndlovu-Gatsheni, 2013), media studies (Moyo, 2020), and communication studies (Shome, 2019). Ultimately, decolonization is rooted in dismantling colonial and imperialist systems that are built into the social, economic, political, cultural, and religious realities of colonized peoples (Glück, 2018; Mohammed, 2021). The process of decolonization therefore requires tremendous work and effort in addressing these injustices. According to Mohan J. Dutta and Mahuya Pal (2020), "The politics of the local, rural, Indigenous struggles in the Global South serves as the basis of theorizing, constructing decolonization as epistemological work in the South, owned by the peoples of the South, serving the goals of the peoples of the South."

Ngũgĩ wa Thiong'o is known widely for discursively engaging issues of decolonization in language, literature, and beyond. In *Decolonising the Mind*, wa Thiong'o (1986) draws attention to the ways the everyday life and lived reality of the colonized subject and the former colony is imbricated in colonial systems. Colonization's central role in the postcolony demonstrates not only the way it is intertwined with ontology, axiology, and epistemology in this society but also the way it has come to be accepted as the banal and mundane in "postcolonial" life. Wa Thiong'o draws our attention to the importance of resisting colonization by pulling our languages, literature, and knowledge systems out of the periphery to which they have been banished. In the field of media studies, it is imperative to examine the "legacies" of colonization by paying attention to what media content on TV, on radio, and in print and digital media is viewed as valid and what media is not.

Language has also been a key organizing factor in hegemonizing media in Africa, where in places like Ghana English-language media is elevated above Indigenous-language media (Mohammed, 2019). Since colonization, Indigenous Ghanaian languages have been debased, while English has been promoted as the language of civilization. This phenomenon prevails today. Anglo-American dominance not only dispossesses Indigenous communities in Africa but also tremendously diminishes the value of knowledge produced by former colonized peoples in other contexts such as Brazil (Albuquerque, 2021). The everydayness of colonization in African communities like Ghana ultimately means that colonial values are embedded in the way we think, how we speak, and how we think about knowledge, our value systems, our cultures, and so on. This everydayness of colonization and imperialism is inextricably linked to knowledge production and research and the general space of academia where colonized knowledges are devalued and knowledge produced by colonizers is presented as the default and the canon against which *othered* knowledges are measured.

While colonization and imperialism have manifested differently in various communities, there remains a very peculiar way in which colonizers impose their values on colonized subjects whether as settler colonizers or as "former" (neo)colonizers. Language is one of the most common ways colonialism and imperialism have been used to dispossess Indigenous communities in Africa, North America, Asia, Latin America, and the Middle East. The transatlantic slave trade remains one of the greatest atrocities to Africans in the diaspora and on the continent, and its effects are still felt today. Colonization and imperialism not only dispossess colonized peoples but also strip them of their identity and humanity. This means that Western ways of knowing are not only valued in the Ghanaian academy but further legitimized by the ways epistemology and pedagogy are treated across educational levels. Therefore, when we make calls for decolonization, it is important for us to not lose sight of how the academy has historically and presently been implicated in colonization and imperialism (Dutta and Pal, 2020; Mohammed, 2021). To understand decolonization, we need to comprehend the roots of colonization. According to Sylvia Tamale (2020, p.7), "Imperialism and capitalism gave birth to colonialism, which has been kindled and sustained by the logic of fraud, lies, brutal repression, pillage, exploitation and manipulation." Efforts at decolonizing knowledge, therefore, need to be foregrounded in this violent history and present while drawing attention to the importance of not only valuing our Indigenous knowledge systems but also highlighting and celebrating their legitimacy in our communities and beyond. Ultimately, to understand African media studies and communication studies, it is imperative to engage with conversations of the evolution of de-Westernizing the discipline (Willems, 2014), paying attention to how these discussions have shaped pedagogy, research, and practice in the field. Throughout this chapter, my discussion of colonialism refers to the postcolonial present of Ghana, which is intertwined with legacies of (neo)colonialism and imperialism. My discussions of colonialism in Ghana are connected to the reality of Global South communities that are settler-colonial states and victims of capitalism and imperialism.

Decolonizing African Methodologies

Decolonization in the academy is a wholistic process of undoing the harm of colonialism and imperialism in the academy and (re)imagining liberatory futures. This undoing of harm and (re)imagining liberation needs to be done pedagogically (in classrooms, in public scholarship, and beyond), epistemologically (in knowledge production), and ontologically (in ways of being). Here I examine the way that methodologies can be decolonized in African media studies while making connections between this process and other areas of communication studies. There is value in drawing on the lived experience of marginalized people in the academy and the experiences of "overresearched" communities in (South) Asia, Latin America, Africa, and Indigenous communities in North America to begin conceptualizing epistemological decolonization (Dutta and Pal, 2020; Peltier, 2018).

In *Decolonizing Methodologies*, Linda Tuhiwai Smith (2012) presents us with tools to understand the violence of research in Indigenous communities, the importance of disrupting the Western canon in knowledge production, and the potential that Indigenous knowledges hold to not only affirm the lived experience of colonized peoples but also dismantle the colonial values embedded in and woven into academia. Decolonizing methodologies involves interrogating systems that elevate Global North knowledge systems over Global South knowledge systems. For example, Tamale (2020, p. 7) asserts that "colonial intellectualism deliberately denigrated Indigenous oral traditions and wisdom as illegitimate methodologies and tools of storing records." In the field of media studies and communication studies, these colonial intellectual value systems have been interrogated by scholars who center Indigenous-language African media and draw on Indigenous knowledge systems to theorize about the field. It is against this backdrop that I reflect on my experiences conducting research and knowledge generation in Dagbanli in Ghana while drawing attention to the way that this epistemological experience shaped and continues to shape my approach to research in Indigenous communities.

Decolonization is followed by indigenization wherein Indigenous African knowledge systems present in languages, proverbs, folktales, folk songs, cultural artifacts, and others are drawn on to conceptualize new frameworks for understanding various phenomena on the continent. Therefore, to produce knowledge utilizing African methodologies, Dani W. Nabudere's philosophy of Afrikology, which "promotes balanced and sustained relationships with all relations including people of other cultures, the environment and the living and non-living," presents us with the tools to conduct research from an Indigenous perspective (Chilisa et al., 2017, p. 332). Legitimizing Indigenous African knowledge in research paradigms is one of several steps toward decolonizing methodologies in the study of African communities. In the next section, I present new insights on my intervention in and contributions to building an African knowledge paradigm grounded in indigeneity and radical African feminist politics.

Toward an African Feminist Autoethnography

African feminisms have provided theoretical, conceptual, and methodological tools to understand the experiences and lived realities of marginalized people in Africa. African feminisms have also provided tools to bridge theory and praxis and to move discourse and practice in feminist spaces toward liberation. In my engagement with African feminisms, I have learned the importance of contextualizing my work in the history and present of my community and grounding my work in the epistemological resources available to do feminism as a scholar and an activist. It is in this work that I was drawn to the potential of theorizing about African communities by pulling from my experiences in community within these spaces. Here, I expand on what I call an African feminist autoethnography, highlighting the ways this framework can be useful for theorizing about African communities in the fields of media studies, communication studies, rhetoric and other related disciplines.

I assert that African feminist autoethnography focuses on the value of drawing on a scholar's experiences in community with knowledge cocreators while reflecting on these experiences and bringing new insights to the phenomenon under study. Although canonical epistemologies have postulated that scholars should not insert themselves into their work in order to maintain "objectivity" (Dutta and Pal, 2020), we have all come to learn that objectivity is socially constructed and that scholars' research ultimately gets filtered through their perspective or positionality, whether or not they are actively detaching themselves from their work. Besides the façade of "objectivity," there is great value in grounding the action of theorizing in the lived reality of marginalized people.

African feminist autoethnography highlights the value of knowledge produced by Africans that is guided by distinctly feminist values. This framework validates the experiences of Indigenous Africans and emphasizes the roles they can play in building knowledge in their communities. Additionally, African feminisms through the concepts of holism, collectivity, and situationality postulate that knowing and creating knowledge is not just an embodied, individuated experience but a socially situated, collective experience (Cruz, 2015). Therefore, the process of producing (auto)ethnographic knowledge is not a personal but a social one. Theorizing from an African feminist autoethnography framework is important because of the ways Africans have been erased in knowledge production on and about their communities. Selina Makana (2018, p. 367) effectively captures this: "Even when African scholars—more precisely African women—document histories of Africans, we have to demonstrate our intellectual prowess in ways that are not expected of white scholars. It is, therefore, not an exaggeration to state that African women are generally ignored as intellectual subjects because our intellectual labor and knowledge production are so easily dismissed in academic spaces."

Here, I expand on the framework and reflect on the way that an African feminist autoethnography can be a driver of decolonizing methodologies in media studies. This framework creates room for a scholar to be self-reflexive while allowing them room for epistemological flexibility (Mohammed, 2021). Here, a scholar is anyone who contributes to knowledge production irrespective of their educational background, whether or not they speak English, and whether or not they have been published. This shifts attention away from seeing participants as objects of knowledge to cocreators of knowledge. Here, African feminist autoethnography allows for such nuances to be revealed.

A scholar is a member of the community who has not only contributed to sustaining Indigenous epistemologies but also worked hard to contribute to its growth and pass on this knowledge to older community members, peers, and younger generations. By this definition, my paternal grandmother, Nma Amamatu, would be considered a scholar due to contributions to Northern Ghanaian, and specifically Dagbaŋ, gastronomy. Similarly, my maternal uncle Sulemana, who draws on and contributes to Dagbaŋ knowledge systems (of ecology and agriculture) in his farming practices and modifies them via experimentation, is a knowledge producer. Alhassan Yushawu Jahanfo, a Dagbanli news journalist in Tamale, is also a scholar given the way he constantly cocreates new language (in Dagbanli) in collaboration with the Dagbaŋ community to write about and present news about concepts that have not yet been conventionalized in Dagbanli vocabulary.

Through reflecting on knowledge practices in my community, I taught myself to unlearn the idea that valid knowledge is produced only in ivory towers and locked away in paywalled journals. Knowledge can be decolonized only if we reexamine who is considered a scholar or a knowledge producer. This reexamination constitutes a disruption of what academia has conventionally presented as valid and legitimate ways of knowing. Before discussing decolonizing methodologies, we need to work toward undoing the notions and conventions that diminish the importance and legitimacy of Indigenous epistemologies, particularly oral epistemologies, in many African communities.

Beyond an epistemological reawakening through autoethnography, I have learned the importance of allowing myself epistemological flexibility. Epistemological flexibility is researchers' ability to allow themselves not only to be guided by their research data when interpreting them but also to break away from the canon and conventions around theories and methods. For many Indigenous scholars, specifically African scholars who study marginalized communities, Western theories tend to be inadequate and often irrelevant to the work that we do. Raka Shome (2019, p. 197) captures this well: "Indeed, there has been a growing recognition for some time now that new tools and epistemologies are needed or existing ones need to be rearticulated to produce new frames of understanding that are informed by the experiences of the Global South, where those experiences are not simply data to be fitted into existing metropolitan theories."

Ultimately, allowing yourself flexibility to customize Northern theories to understand Southern phenomena or dropping Northern epistemologies altogether if they do not fit your framework is a decolonial act. Even more liberatory is starting off an epistemological undertaking by theorizing from the margins and looking to your Indigenous community to provide the conceptual tools to guide this undertaking. An African feminist autoethnographer looks inward first for guidance to understand their community. African feminist autoethnography centers African knowledge systems, is concerned with the way power keeps oppressed peoples at the margins, and is dedicated to doing no harm in the coproduction of knowledge. This chapter expands on the African feminist autoethnography framework while utilizing it to guide a synthesis of the arguments presented throughout the book.

Indigenizing Methodologies

In indigenizing methodologies in research for the book, I intentionally worked toward being critically self-reflexive in knowledge gathering to ensure that I respected my cocreators of knowledge, followed social and cultural conventions, and was sensitive to gender and power dynamics without necessarily projecting judgment on the community. Indigenizing methodologies requires staying cognizant of the fact that Indigenous research paradigms across the world can overlap given the collectivist and communal values, axiologies, epistemologies, and ontologies in these communities (Steinhauer, 2002). I draw connections to these similarities throughout this section. Therefore, as we continue to make calls for decolonization, it is important for us to understand that South-South solidarity worldwide is vital for devising strategies to undo the colonialist, imperialist, and capitalist systems that maintain our collective oppression. Indigenizing methodologies is also concerned with valuing Indigenous ways of knowing and being (Chilisa et al., 2017; Mignolo and Walsh, 2018; Ndlovu-Gatsheni, 2013). In addition to drawing parallels to understand the manifestations of Indigenous knowledge systems among various communities in Africa and the Global South, it is imperative to take note of the nuances and keep in mind the ways these systems manifest in specific communities.

When I worked to coproduce knowledge with my community, I allowed myself to draw on Indigenous philosophies in the community to guide the knowledge-gathering process. Bilchiinsi was my guiding philosophy as I embarked on this epistemological journey. Similarly, ubuntu, which has been extensively unpacked in research methodology in Southern Africa (Chilisa et al., 2017), espouses some of the values in the Bilchiinsi philosophy. Hence parallels can be drawn between philosophies in Western and Southern Africa to ethically and respectfully gather knowledge on the continent. Next, I discuss Bilchiinsi philosophy, presenting it as collectively produced knowledge that I am merely documenting and grounding my scholarship in. My work in this book may be the first time Bilchiinsi is being documented in an academic book, but it supplements the work that has been done by generations of Dagbamba to preserve Dagbaŋ philosophies and transmit them from generation to generation by word of mouth. That there is not much written academic knowledge on Bilchiinsi philosophy points to the legacies of colonialism that have systematically excluded people from Northern Ghana from academia due to systemic issues such as poor educational infrastructure, poverty, ethnic politics, and so on.

Bilchiinsi Philosophy

The Dagbamba (Dagomba) form one of the largest ethnic groups in Ghana and have existed in the country for many centuries. Dagbanli (Dagbani), the language spoken by Dagbamba, is part of the Mole-Dagbaŋ language group, the second largest language group in the country. Dagbanli is taught in schools across the Northern Region and is the major language used on the radio in the Northern Region. Dagbaŋ knowledge systems manifest in health and healing, environmental conservation and agriculture, clothing and fashion, food and gastronomy, and music and language, among others (Mohammed, 2019). The Dagbaŋ Kingdom is organized around a paramountcy held by the Yaa-Naa. Dagbaŋ has a vibrant griot culture whose custodians are drummers and royal praise singers who often perform at marriage ceremonies, naming ceremonies, funerals, festivals, palaces, and so on. Dagbaŋ knowledge systems are closely tied to this vibrant griot culture, and knowledge in this community is transmitted from generation to generation.

In Dagbaŋ philosophies, Bilchiinsi refers to the importance of valuing humanity and holding human dignity sacred (Dagbamba, past and present). If you dedicate your life to the principles of Bilchiinsi and show that you respect each person's human dignity irrespective of their economic standing, social background, gender, cultural background, disability status, religion, and other characteristics, then you would be regarded as a person with high morals and would have reached the peak of practicing humanity you would be called a *bilchina*. People who dedicate their lives to this philosophy are called *bilchininima*. Being regarded as a bilchina is the aspiration of every member of this community.

To be bilchina does not necessarily mean that you have arrived at the destination of Bilchiinsi; rather, you have shown in your interactions with other people and your community that you value their humanity and will continue to value their humanity even after being accorded this recognition. Bilchiinsi is a constant state of doing and acting in ways that support, safeguard, respect, and protect the humanity and human dignity of all. Bilchiinsi is grounded in mutuality and tied to communal values among Dagbamba. At its core, Bilchiinsi is resistant to and interrogates the violence of colonization, imperialism, white supremacy, and heteropatriarchy. It challenges and questions all forms of violence that violate the sanctity of humanity and human dignity. In my aspirations toward Bilchiinsi, I showed respect to research participants, valued their dignity as humans, and cocreated conditions for them to self-express without pressure from me. Beyond drawing on Indigenous Dagbaŋ philosophies, cultural competence is important in ethically engaging Ghanaian communities and cocreating knowledge with historically marginalized Indigenous communities.

Cultural Competence and Knowledge Cocreation

In indigenizing methodologies to study media in African communities, it is important to understand the history of the community and how this history has shaped its contemporary culture and conventions. Although we live in an increasingly globalized neoliberal society, many Indigenous African cultures have maintained and sustained their cultural systems by resisting neoliberalism. Therefore, although the institutional review board (IRB) at American universities provides guidelines for conducting human subjects research, these guidelines do not necessarily emphasize the importance of learning the cultures of communities, following social rules in recruiting research participants, and maintaining long-term relationships with participants (as may be the expectation in some communities). This shortcoming of the IRB is ironic given that it was established because of unethical research practices on African American men in Tuskegee, Alabama (Walker, 2009).

As a member of the community with which I coproduce knowledge, I knew firsthand the importance of following social norms when inviting community members to participate in research, interacting with them in the process of knowledge generation, maintaining an open line of communication with interlocutors, and generally navigating cultural norms. For example, when I entered a community to cocreate knowledge, I first introduced myself by telling them my name, where I was born and raised, and where I lived, and I shared information about my ancestral homes and family. This mode of self-introduction is typical of practices of introduction within this community and enabled interlocutors to get to know me before deciding whether I was worthy of their trust and confidence. This practice, which is prevalent in many collectivist communities in African contexts like Ghana, has also been observed among Indigenous communities in the North America. According to Cindy Peltier (2018), an Indigenous woman who cocreates knowledge with Anishinaabe communities in Turtle Island (North America), community members were interested in knowing her familial ties as part of the process of getting to know her.

Depending on the relative age of interlocutors, I would follow cultural norms of greeting. When I interacted with significantly older interlocutors or people in positions of power such as chiefs, I would squat to initiate the greeting and remain squatting until the greeting concluded and I was excused and asked to sit. In one instance after this introduction and several interactions, an interlocutor told me that as a daughter of the land, it was my responsibility to ensure that the knowledge I gathered was used for good. He also said that unlike white parachute scholars who came into these communities to collect data and then leave and never return, I did not have the luxury of just disappearing since the community knew my family and would follow up to hold me accountable if I tried to pull a disappearing act. Therefore, "as researchers-in-relation, we are often held at a greater level of accountability than a researcher who may not be a member of the community" (Peltier, 2018, p. 5).

Additionally, I followed social conventions by first visiting interlocutors to introduce myself and tell them about my work and how it would affect them and gauge their interest in this knowledge cocreation process. On a second or third visit, I would ask about their level of comfort with being part of the project. Sometimes, interlocutors would agree to have a conversation right away and we would each share knowledge on the topic. At other times, they would propose a future date for this discussion. This process gave them the chance to know me before deciding whether I could be trusted with the knowledge that they might share with me. After we each shared our knowledge on the topic, I would take some time to sit with the knowledge gathered and return to share with them my interpretations of our conversations. Closely related to cultural competence is sensorial listening, which I present as a holistic way of engaging communities with which we cocreate knowledge.

Sensorial Listening in Data Gathering

One of the most important things to consider when conducting media studies research in many West African communities is to do what I call sensorial listening. By sensorial listening I mean listening to the individual interlocutors, interlocutors as a group, and the community and paying attention to how the verbal and nonverbal communication of the interlocutor is situated within the physical, cultural, social, political, and religious landscape of the community. At its core, sensorial listening involves listening with your body and all your senses. It is important to allow your epistemological decisions to be guided by this sort of listening, which is not only an embodied experience but also a physical, cultural, political, and economic experience.

Certain conditions can mitigate an individual or group's communication with the interlocutors, and most of the time this is shaped by the power relations embedded in the community. For example, when I was planning to go to a rural community in the Northern Region to conduct research with men and women about their media consumption habits, I shared my plans with the older people in my family and in the wider community. Some of them asked if men and women would be grouped together for these conversations. When I said yes, they told me that they believed the women would defer to the men if they were put together and asked me to reconsider this choice. Sensorially listening to the larger community about my methodological strategies enabled me to create space for women participants to comfortably share their perspectives without pressure to defer to the men.

When I was conducting research on the film histories of the Northern Region in 2018 for this book, I allowed myself to listen in ways that would let me learn more about the context of the community beyond what I knew from personal and collective memory. In a casual conversation with my mother about this media industry, I learned an important finding about the advertising and publicity practices of this industry in the early 1990s. I quickly noted her comment and followed up on it in my interview with one of the interlocutors who not only confirmed this finding but also recounted his role as a key actor as a poster boy in this process of media advertising and publicity. I discuss this more extensively later in chapter 5. Here again, African feminist autoethnography was tremendously useful since my familial relationship with a community member whose lived reality intertwined with the industry enabled me to learn from her experiences, which were pulled from collective memory.

Beyond sensorially listening to oral narratives, my personal memories of the media industry put into the context of contemporary practices enabled me to reflect on the evolution of media distribution practices, publicity strategies, and marketing strategies. By visiting old sites of media production and distribution such as production studios, distribution stores, and cinema buildings, I was able to place side by side my memories of these sites and how they had changed in recent times. As I went about my daily routine of interacting with family, friends, and community, I began to learn about the ways that media was situated in the physical architecture of this community and how this situatedness shaped other cultural aspects of the community. In this instance, sensorial listening was not only instrumental in using collective memory to understand the media industry, but also useful in facilitating my contextualization of visual media in the past and present of the community. Next, I reflect on my methodological interventions, which were guided by Indigenous philosophies.

The Communal Conversation Circle (CCC)

In gathering knowledge on the politics of Dagbanli film production, distribution, and consumption in 2018, I found myself grappling with the inadequacies of focus group discussions to accommodate the comfort of interlocutors and to pull out the nuances in the narratives that would emerge from these conversations. In the end, I restructured and indigenized the focus group discussion method to center the needs of interlocutors. This is how the communal conversation circle (CCC) emerged when I worked on gathering data on the film viewing habits of rural audiences. Although focus groups are effective for data collection since the methodology aligns with collectivist cultural norms (Amoakohene, 2004), CCCs afforded me the freedom to adjust data gathering to the needs and comforts of interlocutors rather than restricting them to a time limit and stringent focus on the topics to be discussed. This way I learned about the intricacies of film consumption by pulling from the collective memory and experiences of participants.

Although Herbert J. Rubin and Irene S. Rubin (1995) assert that focus groups do not typically follow natural conversation patterns since interlocutors are usually unfamiliar with each other, the CCCs broke this mold because interlocutors were invited to the conversation through a snowball sample, and interlocutors already knew each other and were comfortable interacting with one another. I use the word "invitation" rather than "recruitment" because although the consent of interlocutors was secured to ensure their participation, they were not required to show up or stay throughout the conversation. In this way, the CCCs mirrored conventions of natural conversation in this community.

Inviting interlocutors who already knew each other ensured the creation of an organic conversation among them, thereby facilitating easy discussion. Although the discussions took on some focus group conventions, I employed strategies that made interlocutors comfortable by making these discussions follow the dynamics of natural conversations. If I had strictly followed the conventional focus group model, it would have been difficult to get interlocutors to discuss their feelings about film viewing with total strangers. In such sociocultural contexts, people rarely open up to strangers about personal issues including their positions on socially contentious topics; therefore, I used the CCCs to replicate societal norms in this community. That I was only a moderator and not a participant in the group discussions amplified interlocutors' interests in engaging and joining in the conversation.

The CCC aptly describes these discussions because interlocutors not only were familiar with each other but also had close social and familial relationships and shared cultural experiences. While discussions started with all interlocutors on an equal footing, group leaders emerged organically based on factors such as age, influence in the social group and community, the ways community members related to them, and how CCC interlocutors interacted with and deferred to them. Group leaders usually encouraged other interlocutors to share their perspectives by nudging them and gently pulling them into the conversation. The leaders would put individual interlocutors at ease by asking them to comment on specific films the leader knew they had seen. As the interlocutors talked about their favorite films at length, they would become more comfortable and discuss other related topics. This strategy was important in building not just my rapport with the group but also the members' comfort with each other. These CCCs took place in spaces proposed by group members. These spaces could be the verandah of a house or the private room (hut) of an interlocutor with the door open.

The CCC model, based in Indigenous philosophy, makes a preliminary African feminist intervention in research methods by ensuring that female voices are not erased in conversations. To this end, groups were organized based on gender because, in this context, many formal and informal conversations had a gendered element to them. I arrived at the decision of organizing the CCCs by gender by consulting with my community handler and other members of the larger community about the gender makeup of the CCCs. Many of the community members consulted (both male and female) believed that putting men and women together in a CCC would skew discussions toward a dominant male perspective because many of the female interlocutors would defer to their male counterparts for commentary on topics discussed. Organizing these CCCs by gender proved invaluable to the discussion as interlocutors felt comfortable to discuss film consumption without being distracted/intimidated by power dynamics and/or pressured to adhere to patriarchal hegemonic gender norms that privilege male voices over female voices.

Another reason why these discussions were better run as CCCs is that interlocutors were free to leave the conversation to tend to chores and rejoin later if they wanted. This model mirrored normative conversation patterns within this society. Conversations took place in huts, stores, and other open communal spaces where interlocutors together with the researcher sat in a circle to discuss films and film consumption. Sometimes conversations took place while interlocutors attended to work such as shelling groundnuts, cooking, and minding children. As expected, I often helped by minding children or assisted with the chores that interlocutors engaged in while we conversed.

As in organic conversational contexts within these communities, individuals came and left as they pleased without any obligation to stay for the entire conversation. Interlocutors extensively discussed their consumption of films and sometimes narrated entire plots of films to elicit others' participation. I did not try to curtail their freedoms or bring them back on topic because, per conversational conventions in this community, this might have been perceived by some as impolite. This meant that conversations lasted longer than usual. This free conversation style also created space for me to get to know interlocutors through the stories they told and the tangents they went off on. I was then able to understand the knowledge that they shared within the context of their life stories and experiences. Doing chores during the CCCs ensured that interlocutors did not "lose time" while engaging in these conversations. In the next section, I reflect on how my writing and citation politics are shaped by Indigenous philosophies.

Citing Collectively Produced Knowledge

In graduate programs, the art of writing up research is rarely taught as part of the curriculum. Instead, students are expected to know how to write the literature review, method, and findings sections. There is an assumption that if students make it into graduate school, they arrive with prior knowledge of how to write according to academic styles and conventions. Although some graduate programs offer methods classes that are in some cases required for graduation, very few of these classes actually teach students how to gather data, analyze data, and write up research findings for academic and/or popular audiences. In many graduate classes, the course structure is more focused on content than on how to write or conduct research. For many graduate students who do not have academic parents to teach and mentor them on how to write for publication, it takes years of self-teaching and sometimes external writing groups to learn.

Graduate students therefore operate under the assumption that writing nebulously and interspersing writing with course terminology and big words will demonstrate to their professors that they are engaging in intellectual discourse. This assumption stems from the fact that many readings assigned in graduate classes use inaccessible language, which means that they cannot even be assigned in undergraduate classes or be read and/or understood by people outside the ivory tower. Communicating knowledge should be a skill taught in graduate classrooms. Additionally, graduate curricula should indicate to students that writing in an inaccessible manner is not a marker of "intellectual superiority"; rather, it promotes the exclusionary politics perpetuated by academia and contributes further to making knowledge inaccessible.

My writing has always been guided by the philosophy that if my parents who are not academics (in the traditional sense) are unable to read and understand my work, then I have failed as a scholar to communicate and share my research with the broader society. Therefore, I endeavor to actively *write with* (Mignolo and Walsh, 2018; Smith, 2012) research participants whom I position as cocreators of knowledge in my work. In writing with them, I present their perspectives by sharing quotes from conversations to demonstrate how the data shape the findings instead of largely paraphrasing the data, as is standard practice. This way, interlocutors self-represent instead of being spoken for by me in language that they themselves might find inaccessible. This style guides the way that I present my arguments; interlocutors' voices tremendously support the arguments I make in the book.

Following knowledge gathering, I often went back to interlocutors to share with them an overview of my understanding of the project's findings and to present an opportunity for them to correct any misinterpretations, misrepresentations, and mischaracterizations of their narratives. These conversations were two-way, where community members asked me to share my perspectives and projections about the future of the media industry. In this exercise, I learned tremendously from them and they had the opportunity to learn some things from me. I thus centered the lived experience of the community in studying their engagements with media while utilizing their positionalities to highlight and affirm Dagbaŋ epistemologies.

Ultimately, gathering research data in Dagbanli enabled interlocutors to self-represent and express their ideas comfortably without the pressures of using a language that they might have been uncomfortable communicating in. I was able to sit with the data gathered and reflect on the ways to best translate them into English, the language in which I publish. The challenge with this model was that I had to translate our conversations into English which meant that much of the essence of Dagbanli was lost in translation as I tried to find language to adequately express concepts that often did not exist in English. Nevertheless, holding these conversations in Dagbanli was a subversive act that not only affirmed the interlocutors but also demonstrated to them that I valued their perspectives and Dagbaŋ knowledge systems.

Many calls for de-Westernizing and decolonizing media studies and communication studies have raised issues about citation politics and how this adversely affects the career growth of scholars of color, female scholars, and scholars of color specifically based in the Global South (Chakravartty et al., 2018). The erasure of marginalized scholars in citation practices not only reinscribes the Western canon but also delegitimizes marginalized knowledges. While it is important to be mindful of erasing marginalized scholars in our citation practices, it is important to reflect on the inadequacies of citation conventions in academic knowledge production, which ultimately valuate scholars based on neoliberalist, capitalist systems of hierarchies.

Decolonizing citation practices involves interrogating its imbrication in colonialist, imperialist, capitalist, white supremacist, patriarchal systems wherein individual endeavors of knowledge production are valued above collective efforts of knowledge production. By this, I am not referring to collaborative research projects with several coauthors, wherein the convention is to value solo-authored papers over collaborative/coauthored papers. This phenomenon still demonstrates the capitalist and individualist values of knowledge production in the academy. When I say academia values individual research endeavors over collective knowledge building efforts, I mean that the ivory tower creates the conditions for collective knowledges produced by Indigenous communities (in, for example, African communities) to be co-opted by individual scholars and presented as their personal career achievements and "discoveries" while erasing the collective communal effort that produced these knowledges. The neoliberalist, capitalist academy, which obsesses over issues of copyright, individual achievements of scholars, citation rates, and so on, endorses the erasure of collective knowledge production by communities that struggle to survive under capitalism, (neo)colonization, and imperialism. This manifests as actions such as locking away academic knowledge behind paywalled journals and insisting on an individualist approach to citation.

Therefore, although Indigenous philosophies, axiologies, ontologies, and epistemologies do not subscribe to Western individualist, capitalistic, and neoliberalist ideas about knowledge production, these knowledge systems should not be erased. Journal and (university) press guidelines for citation rarely include guidelines on how to cite *collectively produced knowledge*. I demonstrate this in the earlier section on "Indigenizing Methodologies" by providing a citation that collectively references Dagbamba and Dagbaŋ in my discussion of Dagbaŋ philosophies. I present a model for citing collectively produced knowledge in the bibliography (see Dagbamba, past and present). Journal editors, editorial boards, and reviewers need to more consciously unlearn the colonialist socialization that places the Western canon above all other ways of knowing, especially oral epistemologies.

Beyond Indigeneity as Method and Theory

In this chapter I examined decolonization within the context of knowledge gathering in media studies research in Ghana. I presented various philosophies, concepts, and methodologies to guide African scholars (especially early career scholars) charting their own paths in knowledge production by decolonizing methods, indigenizing knowledge gathering processes, and centering the voices of coproducers of knowledge. I utilized an African feminist autoethnography framework to present my experiences as a researcher and community member in my work that documents the histories and present of a Northern Ghanaian community in relation to media. Theorizing from a decolonial perspective means that scholars hold themselves to the standards that they often hold media producers, distributors, and consumers. Through this framework, we challenge ourselves to disrupt the disciplinary status quo by reflecting on how our work is situated in colonial, capitalist, imperialist systems while working toward engaging Indigenous communities ethically.

While it is important to center Indigenous African ways of knowing in research, it is just as important to note that written knowledge is not superior to oral knowledges. I believe that my work in this book that documents Indigenous knowledges merely supplements the already existing systems of preserving and transmitting knowledge from generation to generation via our lunsi, gonje and others (griots). I demonstrate throughout the book that I am merely a griot documenting the knowledge of my community in an additional, alternative mode.

It behooves African scholars, the fields of media, rhetoric and communication studies, academic departments, conferences, journals, and so on to support the decolonization of knowledge and the legitimization of marginalized ways of knowing to support the self-determination of Global South communities. This can also take the form of creating conditions for Global South scholars to thrive in their journeys to produce knowledge at home and elsewhere. As African scholars who have been socialized to value the Western canon above our own epistemologies (Ndlovu-Gatsheni, 2013), it is important for us to unlearn this socialization and do the work of centering our systems of knowing in our decolonial work. It is our role as knowledge producers to dismantle harmful epistemological systems and build systems to hold parachute scholars accountable so that they do not continue to harm marginalized communities through their cultural incompetence, epistemic violence and Western approaches to research. There is no better time to do that than now.

2

Technology, Literacy, and Media Development in Northern Ghana

●●●●●●●●●●●●●●●●●●●●●●

Biɛla biɛla ndaa nam wɔbgu

For much of my time in high school, I lived in a community that had not yet been connected to electricity. This was a sharp contrast to my early childhood when I lived in a household where I watched programs on Ghana Television (GTV) like *By the Fireside, Teleclass, Toddler's Time,* and *Kwasasa* and had access to some American children's programming such as *The Powerpuff Girls, Dexter's Laboratory, The Flintstones, Johnny Bravo,* and other programs on the Cartoon Network. Here, I was completely cut off from pop-cultural circles where these topics were discussed. Sometimes at school my colleagues would discuss all these new programs and telenovelas they were watching and I had no way to relate to these conversations. Moving to this community gave me a chance to experience firsthand and see the way that many people who lived without electricity spent their days. Before this time, I had only glimpses of this life when I visited my family in Yendi and Zabzugu for the holidays in the late 1990s. Not very far from our house in Tamale across the main road, the other side of the community was connected to electricity. Although communities closer to the central business district of Tamale tended to be connected to power, we were not even though we were not far from the city center.

Although I already had a positive relationship with radio having grown up beside Tamale's first radio station, Radio Savannah, I had an even closer relationship with this medium given the limited options that I had to explore content on other mediums such as television. This was quite the childhood experience because while we still owned a functioning analog color TV set, we couldn't watch television because we were not connected to power. At night I would spend some time studying with the help of a kerosene lantern. My parents worried about the effect that using this lantern would have on my vision. Before long, my father bought a fancy solar-powered, rechargeable lamp that also functioned as a radio set. Thus, even within the same city, within a radius of two and a half miles, my access to media varied because of discrepancies in infrastructural development and electrical connectivity. This is among the many reasons why we cannot speak of a uniform generational experience because levels of accessibility to media in Ghana have often been starkly defined by attendant differences in geographical location, ethnicity, and socioeconomic class. These discrepancies date back to the days of colonization and persist today due to a lack of political will by various governments to address the structural inequities that disproportionately affect the regions of the North. Therefore, in this chapter I argue that to understand the intricacies of media accessibility in the country, it is imperative to interrogate power politics and how that has shaped the lives of many with regard to media access and connecting to the national public sphere. I share these personal experiences to provide the larger context for the wide disparity in technological, media, and literacy access between Ghana's North and South.

This chapter foregrounds the main argument of the book by contextualizing media development and growth in Northern Ghana by highlighting how infrastructure like electricity access and literacy shaped media access and the citizenry's participation in the national public sphere. I begin by discussing electrical connectivity and how it laid the foundations for the growth of local radio, film, and television. My focus on radio, television, and the internet in this chapter draws attention to the structural factors that shape media access, growth, and development in Northern Ghana. Building on this, I discuss the evolution of media growth and access in the Northern Region with regard to media development in Ghana. I discuss the evolution of media in the region and nation in detail in subsequent chapters. Although there is existing research on radio, television, film, and the internet in Ghana, there hasn't been much focus on making the connections between media accessibility and structural marginalization focusing specifically on Northern Ghana.

The first public electricity grid came to Ghana in 1914 through Sekondi (IDE-JETRO, n.d.) but it wasn't until 1989 that Northern Ghana by way of Tamale was connected to the national grid for public consumption (Yamusah, 2013). The Volta River Authority (VRA) and the Northern Electrification Department (NED) worked to maintain electricity access in the region. And even though the North was connected to the national grid in 1989, many communities within the Tamale area were still not connected until the mid-2000s. Similarly, it would take some time for many rural communities of what is now known as the other four regions of the North to be connected to electricity. This late arrival of power access also meant that it took quite a while for TV technology to diffuse across the region. In my community in Zogbeli, ours was one of the few houses with a color television set in the early 1990s. Many households had black-and-white TVs. Compare this to the invention of color television in 1928 and you will understand how innovations are diffused in the Global South versus the Global North and how this parallels the conversations on the digital divide today in Africa. Despite the tremendous growth the country has seen in power connectivity, several communities in the country have yet to be connected to electricity. And of course electricity access can be mapped onto geographical location, ethnicity, and socioeconomic class. Therefore, the closer a region is to the national capital, the closer it is to development and to the dividends of the national development agenda.

In the early 2000s, we had moved from our rented chamber and hall in Zogbeli to our own three-room compound house in Tamale South. Although our new place was about a ten-minute drive from the central business district, we were still not connected to power. This was the reality of many people living in proximity to the central business district of Tamale. It therefore took a while for communities farther from Tamale to connect to the national grid. Although a little over 40 percent of the national population had access to electricity in the 2000s, the connectivity rate in 2021 had increased significantly to about 86 percent (International Trade Administration, 2022). The connectivity rate may however be lower across the five regions of the North, which due to structural factors have trailed behind the national average on all neoliberal development metrics. The marginalization of the North today can in fact be traced to social, political, economic, and historical factors such as slavery and colonialism, whose effects still reverberate through the region today (Saboro, 2022).

According to musician and scholar Sheriff Ghale (who produces knowledge under his given name, Mohammed Sheriff Yamusah), the connection of Tamale to electricity in 1989 tremendously shaped the growth of the media industry in the region (Yamusah, 2013). This development not just greatly shaped the region in the area of media but also opened up the North to slow industrial and infrastructural development (Yamusah, 2013). We can therefore draw connections between the North's late arrival to electricity access and media framings and public discourses that construct the North as backward and uncivilized. Electricity access not only propelled development and industrialization in Ghana but also brought the country into the space of the global public sphere even if as mere spectators. This can be extrapolated to understand the situatedness of Northern Ghana in various conversations in the public sphere. Before this historical milestone, Northerners were merely spectators of development and media growth in the country. This connection to electricity opened up avenues for the growth of the music and film industries in the region. By extension, the North was systematically excluded from actively participating in the Ghanaian public sphere, among others. Ultimately, there is a strong connection between technology, media, and literacy in facilitating the development of not just the North but the country as a whole. And studying these connections can help us understand why the North is disproportionately disadvantaged as far as digital access is concerned.

Literacy and Education in Northern Ghana

Although we are seeing growth in television access, smartphone use, and social media subscriptions, we need to understand this growth within the larger context of literacy and education in Ghana. Current demographic data on literacy, education, and standards of living will present a clearer picture on where Ghana and the North stand with regard to digital access. According to the latest population and housing census, conducted in 2021, while Ghana's national literacy rate is about 70 percent, the Northern Region's literacy rate is about 41 percent, one of the lowest regional literacy rates in the country (Ghana Statistical Service, 2022b). These data demonstrate that a large portion of the population in the region does not have the tools to engage in literary media in English or Indigenous Ghanaian languages. The situation is no different in the area of educational access and levels of educational attainment. The same census data demonstrate that people living in the Northern part of the country are less likely to complete education up to high school and junior high school (Ghana Statistical Service, 2022a). The situation is even more dire at the postsecondary level, where many drop out and are unable to make it to universities, professional schools, and postsecondary technical and vocational institutions. We see some of this lack of access to resources for quality education at programs like the *National Science and Maths Quiz*, which often highlights the country's elite schools concentrated in the Central, Greater Accra, Ashanti, and other regions of the South. Therefore, when access to formal education is used as a tool to measure infrastructural and human resource development, the North often lags behind.

Ghana (previously the Gold Coast) was under British colonial rule from the 1800s to 1957; the British colonizers determined which regions were deserving of a Western education and which were not. Regardless of which nation colonized the Northern Territories (now known as Northern Ghana) at any given time, this region was often excluded from educational, social, political, and infrastructural development. This structural marginalization of the North was carried into postcolonial Ghana and persists today. It is therefore unsurprising that while Ghana's first secondary school (Mfantsipim

School) was established by colonial missionaries in 1876 in the now Central Region, Northern Ghana's first secondary school (now Tamale Senior High School) opened in 1951. During this time the Gold Coast was a colony, not a nation, but the various regions and territories were gradually incorporated to make it one colonial unit and eventually a nation. I use secondary education to illustrate this inequality because it is the level of education that produced students who could make it into the formal employment sector such as the civil service. Today, it is virtually impossible to secure a civil service job without any postsecondary education. While there were primary schools in the North as early as the 1900s, it wasn't until the 1950s that Northern students could get a secondary education in their region (Staniland, 1975).

It is therefore unsurprising that only one Northern secondary school, St. Francis Xavier Junior Seminary, has ever made it to the finals of the much-coveted *National Science and Maths Quiz* (National Science and Maths Quiz, n.d.). In fact, no school from the North has ever won this quiz competition since its inception in 1993 (National Science and Maths Quiz, 2023). Not only are Northern institutions underfunded and underresourced, there have been inadequate efforts on the part of government to make educational access equitable across the country.

Beyond the educational inequities, the North is systematically annihilated in media and literary representations in the country. There is very little representation of stories and narratives about the North in Ghana's literary scene, which is based in Accra. This lack of representation can be traced to the historical disenfranchisement of this region. Apart from authors such as Ayesha Harruna Attah, Susannah Alhassan, Portia Dery, G. A. Agambila, and a few others who have worked on fictionalized narratives that represent the rich tapestry of the cultures of the North, there isn't much representation of this half of Ghana on the literary scene. Academics and historians such as lawyer Ibrahim Mahama, the late Zoosali Lana Tia Sulemana, and others have documented the histories of Northern communities focusing disproportionately on the royal histories of the Dagbamba. These histories have been told from a male perspective, which means that women who contributed in myriad ways to these communities are erased from historical accounts of their communities.

Other historical narratives of the region that capture the lives of Northerners have often been documented by white Africanists like Martin Staniland, Wyatt MacGaffey, and others who often need the help of translators to do this work. This means that these accounts are seldom reliable not only because the scholars do not have direct access to the language but also because of the coloniality that often drives the scholarly agenda of anthropologists, "Africanists," and other scholars of Africa who engage the continent through a colonial gaze. Although we are seeing a gradual surge in Northerners from lower-middle-class and working-class communities in academia who are working to fill these gaps in building epistemologies from the perspective of formerly colonized communities, more work needs to be done to ensure that the full complexities of subaltern communities are captured in the history building process. That is, perspectives that are not dominated by the Ghanaian colonial elite class who often reproduce coloniality in the ways that they engage and represent marginalized communities. An understanding of oppression in Ghana would require us to consider the way that geographical location, ethnicity, socioeconomic class and gender intertwine to shape the power dynamics around history making (Mohammed, 2023b).

Although African American scholars like Patricia Hill Collins (2009) and Kimberlé Crenshaw (1991) have theorized power and oppressive structures through concepts like the "matrix of domination" and "intersectionality," respectively, many global scholars were already examining identity from multiple perspectives. Collins and Crenshaw's scholarship, however, provided the precise language to effectively theorize identity and power structures. We are seeing a growth in scholarship in the Global South that is being inspired by and draws from these epistemological traditions. In re-righting the subaltern histories of Ghana, I situate and foreground my identities as a woman, Dagbana, and Muslim to write marginalized communities into these national narratives. Therefore, intersectionality and the matrix of domination not only are useful for theorizing and understanding various identities, but also open pathways toward rethinking what epistemological disruptions to foreground the margins can look like. May (2015, p. 35) captures this succinctly: "By unmasking knowledge claims purported to be neutral and universal, [intersectionality] raises questions about who has been perceived to be an authoritative knower, whose claims have been heard, which forms of knowledge have received recognition (and been recorded, archived, and passed down), and who has had access to the means of knowledge production and training (including access to education, the academy, and publishing)." The arguments I present in this chapter draw attention to the structural marginalization of Northern Ghana, highlighting the region's situatedness in discourses around education and academic knowledge production.

Ultimately, the histories around literacy are interconnected with the histories of Western education and the propagation of the Christian gospel in Ghana. This means that literacy and education cannot be extricated from media access and media consumption because newspapers such as *The Daily Graphic* have served English-speaking audiences since their inception. Most radio programming from the Ghana Broadcasting Corporation (GBC) has served English audiences, even though there were efforts to transmit in a few selected Indigenous languages. The print media industry has also historically been based in Accra, which means that there weren't and still aren't many local English newspapers in various regions across the country, let alone newspapers published in Indigenous Ghanaian languages. Since Ghana inherited a colonial education system based on English as the medium of instruction, Indigenous languages have been sidelined and literacy programs in Indigenous Ghanaian languages have not seen much support. Therefore, the educational system has taken a lax attitude toward teaching Ghanaian languages while investing efforts in teaching English and using it as the medium of instruction in many levels of the educational ladder.

Organizations such as the Ghana Institute of Linguistics, Literacy and Bible Translation (GILLBT) therefore took it upon themselves to promote Ghanaian language literacy in local communities (Aggoh and Siabi-Mensah, 2003). Although GILLBT's first mandate was to promote Bible translation and literacy development for the propagation of Christianity, they soon expanded their operations beyond religion. It is imperative therefore to contextualize GILLBT's work in supporting the development of Ghanaian language literacy against Christianity's history of and current complicity in the Euro-American colonial project. GILLBT took on the important project of promoting Indigenous-language literacy especially among communities whose languages were endangered because they were classified as minority languages. Minority languages have small populations, which means that these languages are rarely represented in the public sphere and are almost never taught in schools. GILLBT has focused on what they call "mother tongue literacy" development. Through their projects, they have created space for documentation and literary development in communities that are often underserved (Aggoh and Siabi-Mensah, 2003). GILLBT's work in translating minority languages into the literary space fills the gap where dominant languages often take up space in the public sphere via media and Western education. This organization clearly understands that language and culture are inextricably linked. Therefore, providing Christian texts in Indigenous languages brings the religion in close proximity to culture and develops and maintains a strong bond between the religion and the culture embedded in these languages. While these efforts are driven by a Christian organization whose main interests lie in pushing a Christian agenda onto the culture making process, it is imperative to note that "mother tongue literacy" is tied to identity formation and (re)negotiation, self-determination, and agency. Although most literacy projects often target children and youth, GILLBT's programs identify the gaps in literacy where adults are often excluded and focus on adult literacy. Beyond promoting Christianity, literacy projects such as GILLBT's have supported civic engagement for disenfranchised communities in rural areas. In a conversation with Peter Wangara Amoak, director for literacy, education, and development at GILLBT, I learned more about the expansive nature of GILLBT's literacy programs: "We have produced loads and loads of materials on various topics on health, on civic awareness, rights, and the rights of people, especially the Ghanaian woman, the Ghanaian child. We've translated the Constitution, you know. And, of course, we also need to preserve our traditional customs. So, we have books on traditional stories. We have books on riddles. Oh, so much material, these various local languages, so much. And that is what actually won us the prize from UNESCO" (February 2023). One of GILLBT's literacy projects that supported a more informed public and a vibrant public sphere was their collaboration with the National Commission for Civic Education in which they translated an abridged version of the 1992 Ghana Constitution into twenty-four Indigenous languages (Aggoh and Siabi-Mensah, 2003). These projects often emphasize community engagement and involvement, ultimately instilling in community members a sense of ownership of the products of the literacy projects of the organization. We cannot argue for the importance of developing African languages without drawing attention to the dearth of publishing resources in the area. In Africa, there are very few publishers who are committed to the production of knowledge in African languages. A few are Mkuki na Nyota, a Pan-African Tanzanian publisher that publishes in Swahili, East African Educational Publishers, which has done work in Kikuyu, and GILLBT, which publishes across a wide spectrum of Ghanaian languages. More work therefore needs to be done to promote the development of a publishing culture that captures the complexities and nuances of African cultures and languages.

Beyond Indigenous-language publishing, I provide a larger context for understanding the linguifam and linguicide that minority languages face. According to wa Thiong'o (2009), linguifam is the starving of a language through colonial processes that place the language at the bottom of the linguistic hierarchy, hence not developing literary forms of the language, which might lead to its eventual death—linguicide. Ghana has over seventy languages, but only eleven of them are taught in schools. The languages that are taught are classified as major languages and are often taught at the primary and junior high levels, ideally to every child. To learn an Indigenous language at the high school level, a student must select it as an elective subject. Usually, the dominant language of the region is taught in school. For example, Dagbanli is taught in the Northern Region, Gonja in the Savannah Region, Ewe in the Volta Region, and so on. Despite these efforts at promoting Indigenous-language education, only a negligible number of Ghanaians are literate in their first language, although they may have high levels of oral fluency in these languages. The reason can be attributed to what Ngũgĩ wa Thiong'o (1986) calls a colonization of the mind, where Africans are brainwashed to be disdainful of their own languages while putting European colonial languages on a pedestal. And this disdain is structural since it is taught in school together with the Westernization process that African children are subjected to in their quest for education. This colonization of the mind through language stripped away more than Africans' linguistic identity, including their dignity, heritage, memory, and history. "In the African continent, African languages—deprived of the food, water, light, and oxygen of thought, and of the constant conceptualizing that facilitates forging of the new and renewal of the old—underwent slow starvation, linguifam" (wa Thiong'o, 2009, p. 19). Wa Thiong'o's observation of the slow death of African languages not just demonstrates the current implications of colonization and neocolonialism on the African continent but is reminiscent of the globality of colonialism and imperialism, bringing to mind the similar fate of Indigenous communities such as the Māori of New Zealand and the many Indigenous communities of the Americas. It is therefore imperative to make connections between the struggles of various Global South communities in order to work toward a decolonial praxis that can be localized for each sociocultural and geopolitical context.

A Colonized Mind or a Colonial Curse?

When I was a student at the University of Ghana, where I studied, English, Spanish, and sociology, I learned about the depth of the colonization of our minds when our Spanish lecturer in the third year, Dr. Lamptey, posed a question to the class: How many of you will speak only English to your children in the future? Most of the students in the class raised their hands. With an expression of disappointment on his usually happy and jovial face, he proceeded to gently reprimand the class about the dangers of elevating English and other European languages over Ghanaian languages and how it was important for each and every one of us to pass on our proficiency and knowledge about our respective languages to our children to ensure that our languages were not subjected to the linguifam and linguicide that wa Thiong'o speaks about. It is not lost on me that this education on decolonizing our minds and working to contribute to the development of Ghanaian languages happened in a class where we were being taught a European language. This is a subject to unpack another day.

What we learn from this incident is that this manner of thinking that denigrates African languages is ingrained in us from infancy. As soon as we start school, we are taught that our languages are local and therefore useless in the global world. It was not lost on me that the languages that were taught in the Department of Modern Languages included only a single African language, Swahili. No Ghanaian language was taught in this department as a modern language. The languages taught were and still are Swahili, Spanish, Russian, Arabic, and Chinese. French is a whole department on its own. While these languages formed majors that students chose to pursue, usually at the undergraduate level, Ghanaian languages such as Dagbanli, Twi, Ga, and Ewe were taught by the Institute of African Studies as options for students who chose the language option in order to complete the compulsory African studies course requirement for all students. I studied Ga to fulfil my African Studies requirements during my undergraduate study. Students who chose the music or dance option to fulfil this requirement could avoid learning a Ghanaian language altogether. Today, many middle-class Ghanaian parents pride themselves on taking their wards to international schools, run on international curricula that rarely teach Ghanaian histories and knowledges, let alone Ghanaian languages. In some of these schools, students are indoctrinated to elevate European languages while denigrating their own mother tongues. Here, they can learn languages such as French and Spanish. Their knowledge of other subjects is grounded in a mainly British or American curriculum. In fact, these schools not only service the wards of the Ghanaian elite class but provide a purely Western education to the wards of the expatriate class. Students leave these schools having extensive knowledge to become Afropolitans who are essentially global citizens. These kids usually have a chance to vacation in the imperial core to supplement their knowledge of Western cultural events such as Coachella, Burning Man, Comic Con, Halloween, and others. It is unsurprising therefore that knowledge about Global North pop culture and other cultural events boosts the cultural capital of Afropolitans who find themselves feeling at home almost anywhere in the world.

Afropolitanism is a concept that was popularized by Taiye Selasi, an author and British global citizen of Ghanaian and Nigerian origin, to articulate her experiences as an African who moves seamlessly across continents. Afropolitanism is a blending of the words "Africa" and "cosmopolitanism" to articulate the unique experiences of the global African elite class (Selasi, 2005). While Afropolitanism is useful for describing the privileges enjoyed by Africa's global elite class, it is imperative to pay attention to not only the way that it operates as a concept that is reactionary to racist and colonialist imaginations of the African continent in the Global North public sphere but also the way that it is shaped by the white Western gaze. Since Afropolitanism is grounded in reacting to and mimicking Western values, it makes sense that this identity is rooted in consumerism and commodification and is beholden to global capitalist values. Afropolitanism therefore centers the experiences of the Afropolitan privileged class while erasing the experiences of majority of Africans on the continent and African immigrants in the global public sphere (Dabiri, 2014; Mohammed, 2025). While discussions on African media often center Afropolitan experiences by, for example, celebrating the nomination of African movies at the Oscars or African music at the Grammy Awards, African movies being streamed on Netflix, and so on, in this project I am interested in understanding and highlighting the experiences that everyday Africans have with media and popular culture. These relationships that Africans have with media in their communities enable us to understand the ways in which culture evolves without being fixated on how the West captures these media cultures through a colonial gaze, commodifies them, and sells them back to the Afropolitan class and the global cosmopolitan class.

Recently, Ghana's Year of Return program, a project that seeks to create the conditions for Africans in the diaspora to reconnect with their homeland and learn their roots, has inspired renewed interest in the continent. The Year of Return was instituted in 2019 by the Nana Addo–led conservative government. According to the program's website, it "celebrates the cumulative resilience of all the victims of the Trans Atlantic Slave Trade who were scattered and displaced through the world in North America, South America, the Caribbean, Europe and Asia" (Year of Return Ghana 2019, n.d.). While this project looks good on paper and has the potential to connect the African diaspora to their homeland, this iteration of it centers on neoliberal and capitalist values focusing instead on how the Ghana government can make money from diasporic Africans' desire to connect with their roots. This iteration of the Year of Return is stripped of the essence of radical liberatory and Pan-African praxis that should underpin the project. The project focuses on trade and investments that the diaspora can explore in Ghana rather than creating the conditions for diasporic Africans to meaningfully connect with their homeland.

This particular project is rooted in Afropolitan values and praxes, which means that everyday Ghanaians become a backdrop in the discourses around the Year of Return. This project not only reproduces elitism but also rehistoricizes the narratives of enslavement in Ghana by completely erasing from this project the North, where many enslaved people who trace their roots to Ghana had their ancestors captured. Instead, slavery narratives center the dominant Asante culture, which not only benefited economically from these indignities that Africans were subjected to but was itself complicit in the process of enslavement (Saboro, 2022). These narratives have been subsumed in Ghanaian histories because the writers of these histories have often come from dominant ethnic groups and have had the chance to (re)write slavery narratives to downplay their role in this painful part of our histories. The Year of Return project has attracted the African American elite class and has seen celebrities such as Gabrielle Union, Dwyane Wade, Beyoncé, Cardi B, and others visit Ghana. Conversations in December—the peak period when diasporic Africans return—often focus on pop culture such as music, films, art, and so on. While these are important sites for understanding the complicated histories around enslavement in Africa, these discourses often focus on the entertainment side of things. In fact, the average Ghanaian may not even know of the Year of Return program. If everyday Ghanaians are not aware of this program, how do they even consciously work to connect with their long-lost siblings who return home? Very often, panels are convened to discuss the hottest music, movies, and other entertainment trends, and the panelists are usually Afropolitans in these sectors who return home to take part in the festivities. Here again, Ghanaians living in Ghana are cast as spectators to if not the backdrop of conversations on Ghanaian histories and identities. Ghanaians in the Northern part of the country often do not even get the chance to be spectators of these conversations. These conversations again are usually grounded in neoliberalism and capitalist values. Over a period of three years (2019–2022), the North has been systematically excluded from the Year of Return festivities, even though many enslaved people were captured from the North. Northern scholars and activists have drawn attention to this irony, and we are beginning to see in 2023 pockets of efforts at including the North in these neoliberalist and capitalist celebrations of the Return of our siblings from the diaspora: "Indeed, northern Ghana is beginning to contest 'the politics of exclusion' in the burgeoning tourist industry in Ghana by trying to reposition herself and become part of the global discourse on the slave trade which has hitherto remained the exclusive preserve of the South" (Saboro, 2022, p. 51). However, there is some hope. In March 2023 while I was in Ghana, I watched the replay of an interview on Pan-African TV (whose CEO is veteran journalist Kwesi Pratt Jnr) where American rapper Noname was discussing socialism, U.S. imperialism, and Pan-Africanism with Kwesi Pratt Jnr and the host Ama Pratt (daughter of Kwesi). These conversations were reminiscent of the connections that African Americans such as Malcolm X, Maya Angelou, W. E. B. Du Bois, and others had with their siblings in Ghana right after the country fought for liberation from British colonization. At this time, connections were made between the independence movements in Africa and the civil rights movement in the United States, demonstrating the globality of the oppression that Africans at home and in the diaspora were subjected to. It is hoped that as more attention is drawn to the superficial nature of the current programming of the Year of Return, more diasporic Africans will seek out spaces where they can connect with everyday Ghanaians and learn about our cultures, about our revolutionary histories, and about how colonialism and imperialism affect Africans at home and in the diaspora. I discuss the systematic exclusion of Northern Ghana from the Year of Return project to illustrate the structural ways in which the North has been erased from the national public sphere even when the histories of slavery directly affected the peoples of the North. The point I make here is that we cannot write the radical histories of Ghana without paying attention to work done by the Ghanaian masses at the grassroots level to support liberation efforts. Indigenous-language media and knowledges hold tremendous potential to rekindle and sustain Africa's relationship with her diaspora.

Afropolitanism and Language Politics

While we debate whether or not Afropolitanism is an identity that many Africans can relate to, we lose sight of the more important conversations that need to be happening around the development and promotion of African cultures through language. It would seem that the experiences of African children in colonial-era schools where they were systematically stripped of the essence of their culture through a de-linguicization and re-linguicization process that annihilated African languages and put European languages in their place is still happening in our current neocolonial reality. Similar processes of de-linguicization were violently imposed on communities in other Global South areas that were colonized and among Indigenous communities in North America. Although we have seen the role of the African elite class in this deculturation and de-linguicization process, this colonial project has been taken a step further where African ways of being are being discarded for the status that comes with proximity to colonial cultures. For example, a *BBC News* story from September 2023 indicated that there is a growing trend among Nigeria's elite class to pay for British accent classes to "polish" their English speech (Orjinmo, 2023). These classes essentially teach Nigerians how to speak like their former colonizers: the British. Never mind that Nigeria is a former British colony that has English as an official language and Nigerian Pidgin English as a lingua franca. This development shows us that there is more work to be done to decolonize the minds of Africans with regard to the hierarchies they have been indoctrinated with at schools where English is elevated above Indigenous languages.

While we grapple with the way that the process of colonization stripped Africans of their self-worth, causing some to even mimic colonizers in speech as seen in the *BBC* story, we have to draw connections between these individual examples and the structural issues that work to starve and undercut the growth and development of African languages. Structural issues are embedded in the various institutions of African countries. This lack of dedication to the development of African languages is structural and is replicated in the media space where Ghana cannot boast of newspapers in Ghanaian languages that are circulating in local communities. Even if resources were put into supplementing GILLBT's work on translating Ghanaian languages into literary forms, there would need to be work on the back end to promote Ghanaian language literacy among community members. Ironically, in the past decade, there has been steady growth in commercial media organizations in radio and TV that transmit in Ghanaian languages. Even though this means that the language can grow and evolve in the media space, there is still a gap in the literary space because many of these media organizations do not even produce broadcast scripts in Indigenous languages. So even though these languages are being grown and nurtured in oral forms, there is no corresponding work in the literary space to document these developments.

Building on wa Thiong'o's discussion of linguicide and linguifam (2009), I present literacide and literafam as the systematic erasure and undermining of the growth of African languages in literary forms (literafam), which may result in their literary death (literacide). Although, there was wide interest from NGOs like School for Life in promoting Indigenous languages like Dagbanli and Likpakpaln among adult learners, there are very few efforts today to sustain this work. Therefore, existing literature on Indigenous languages especially in the North was written decades ago with very few books and pamphlets coming out in recent times to promote language literary development. Therefore, as we are seeing fewer and fewer efforts to promote language literary development, languages are starved of literary growth (literafam) and eventually die off in the literary space (literacide). So while many languages in Ghana are at threat of literafam and literacide, they may be seeing some growth and development in the area of orality. This complicated relationship that the mediascape has with Ghanaian languages is a legacy of colonialism. Media organizations are therefore strategically positioned to collaborate with institutions of higher learning and publishing houses such as GILLBT to promote the development and literary growth of Indigenous languages. In chapter 1, I demonstrated the importance of theorizing Ghanaian media from an Indigenous perspective, highlighting the potential Indigenous knowledges hold to imagine liberatory futures. In subsequent chapters, I point out the connections between Indigenous-language media and African knowledge systems.

Radio and Television in Northern Ghana

Radio and television have come to be established as integral parts of not just the Ghanaian mediascape but the Ghanaian public sphere. Although radio and TV in the country today have taken on more participatory elements with programming that invites audience participation, it wasn't so at their inception. Radio was invented in 1901 and did not see wide adoption by the American masses until the 1930s. It was around this time, in 1935, that radio was introduced to Ghana. The Ghana Broadcasting Corporation (GBC) was established the same year (Blankson, 2005). TV, on the other hand, was invented in 1927 and became widely adopted in American households by the 1950s. Television came to Ghana in 1965, and GBC held a monopoly over the medium until the 1990s. Even though TV and radio innovations took a few decades to reach Ghana, it took even longer for the media industry to be liberalized and for the North to participate in the growth of this mediascape. For decades, Ghanaians were limited to GBC for all broadcast media content until the airwaves opened up in 1995 (Blankson, 2005) and university campus radio like Radio Univers and privately owned commercial media organizations such as Joy FM and TV3 began to operate. In this section, we learn about the diffusion of broadcast innovations in the country and draw parallels between these diffusions and the North's situatedness in these media developments and evolutions.

Although newspapers were circulating in the North before the establishment of local radio stations, access to this medium was limited by English literacy, so the majority of the population of the North at the time were not avid readers of newspapers. The establishment of GBC's Radio Savannah in 1996 revolutionized the media landscape in the region. Therefore, although a handful of the population owned radio sets and were tapped into radio networks before the establishment of Radio Savannah, the establishment of this station made radio a thing for the masses. Everyday people could listen to radio communally even if they did not own radio sets. I witnessed this communal consumption of radio in my community when households would buy radio sets and turn up the volume for the entire compound to listen to a favorite program.

Before long, private commercial stations such as Diamond FM and Fiila FM were established, providing a variety of programming for audiences in Tamale and beyond. In June 2002, there were fifty FM stations on air across the country, but only five of them were distributed across then three regions North—two in the Northern Region, one in the Upper East Region, and two in the Upper West Region (Alhassan, 2005). Even though the Northern Region had a higher population than the Volta, Brong Ahafo, Central, and Western Regions at the time, each of these regions had more FM radio stations than the Northern Region (Alhassan, 2005), again highlighting the structural marginalization of the North in the media sector. Today, there are over twenty radio stations broadcasting out of Tamale alone, meaning that radio is reaching a level of saturation in the region where revenue generation is undermined since many stations are competing for business in a small market. Even when these two commercial radio stations were established, Radio Savannah still occupied an integral position in the Northern Region's mediascape because it had a wider coverage area in the region than these stations whose broadcasts were often limited to Tamale. Local radio has worked tremendously to support civic education and civic engagement not just in the Northern Region but across the country (Andani and Antwi-Boateng, 2021; Mohammed, 2019). For a community that was rarely affirmed in the Ghanaian mediascape for decades, the establishment of Radio Savannah and community radio stations such as Simli Radio has done tremendous work to preserve the cultures of communities that have historically been marginalized and excluded from formal accounts of Ghanaian histories. According to Al-hassan and colleagues (2011), programs on Simli Radio such as *Yung Dema Saha* and *Salma Saha* reimagined traditional customs and forms of entertainment on radio. For example, *Salma Saha* replicated the nighttime storytelling culture of Dagbamba, which was used as a tool to educate younger members of society while grounding them in the values of their community.

Through radio, issues of concern to the local community such as agriculture, health, the environment, and education were brought to the doorstep of the populace, and the conditions were created for community ownership of these issues through participatory radio in the form of phone-in segments of radio shows and listener clubs that community radio stations like Simli Radio supported (Al-hassan et al., 2011). Beyond civic participation, radio contributed to the development of the languages of transmission such as Dagbanli and Gonja. By this I mean that formalized varieties of these languages became part of the public sphere even though these languages were not seeing much development and therefore undergoing literacide. This also means that across the nation dominant languages with majority populations enjoyed the privilege of development in the media and minoritized languages were further disenfranchised. For example, it was rare to find radio stations transmitting in languages such as Bimoba and Basare, which have significant populations in the Northern Region. While scholarly conversations in the Global North grapple with the death of radio and the rise of the podcast industry, radio still occupies an integral position in Africa's mediascape. Across Ghana for example, radio is still one of the main sources of news and current affairs programming, while TV is conceptualized more as an entertainment medium. Later, I will discuss the relationship between radio and development communication within this sociocultural context. With regard to media, radio will always be Tamale's first love because it was the site where participatory communication was developed and a variety of programming was presented for the audiences. It wasn't until 2004 that Metro TV began to transmit in Tamale and then TV3 followed later.

Today, stations like GBC's GTV and private commercial TV such as TV3 and Joy Prime TV are widely available on satellite TV or digital terrestrial free-to-air TV, but for many people in the Northern Region these stations are useful for specific programming, such as morning shows, news bulletins, political programs (like Joy FM's *News File*), and some select entertainment programs like *Ghana's Most Beautiful*, *Date Rush*, and others. More and more people in this community are interested in the new satellite TV stations that transmit in their language. One of the earliest TV stations in the Northern Region was Discovery TV (established in the 2010s), which is now defunct. NTV came in to serve the needs of the populace and satisfy a hunger in this community for affirming television media content that has not been felt for decades. NTV was established in 2015 and for years enjoyed a monopoly as the only TV station in Ghana that transmitted mostly in Dagbanli. Before long, Sagani TV and Zaa TV were established in 2017 and 2021, respectively. Later in the book, I demonstrate the way that satellite TV is situated in Ghana's mediascape today, foregrounding this discussion in the work of Zaa TV, Sagani TV, and NTV.

The Internet and Legacy Media

Although we are seeing new and innovative ways in which the internet has been used to foster a vibrant public sphere in Ghana, we cannot underestimate the integral role that legacy media platforms like TV, radio, and print play in the country's civic space today. While radio is being decried as a dying medium in the Global North (Daugherty, 2022), it remains important in the African mediascape for various reasons, key among which is accessibility. In the Ghanaian context today, beyond accessibility, the media landscape is structured in such a way that radio is the go-to medium for news and current affairs programming. Television is just recently catching up to that sector since TV has been perceived by many in the country as a medium for entertainment. It is important to note that the liberalization of the airwaves in Ghana has contributed to the clear assignment of uses and gratifications to the various media platforms. For example, the most popular television programs across the country, such as *Ghana's Most Beautiful* and *Date Rush*, are entertainment programs, while the most popular radio programs, *Alhaji & Alhaji*, *News File*, *Citi News*, and *Joy News*, are current affairs or news programs. We are seeing growing interest in the morning shows of TV stations that have large portions of their programming dedicated to current affairs discussions.

In discussing the evolution of media, we have to make connections between media growth and media convergence since most media organizations maintain a vibrant online presence through blogs and social media pages. More recently, media organizations that started as radio platforms have expanded to establish TV stations and we are seeing an interesting convergence of TV and radio where programs that were originally made for radio, such as *News File* at Joy FM, are now broadcast as TV programs and transmitted on the radio platforms of these media organizations. Other stations such as Zaa TV are streaming their programs on their Facebook page to reach not just audiences on the platform who are located in Ghana but also the Ghanaian community in the diaspora. Other Accra-based radio stations are transmitting programs live on Twitter Spaces, while TV stations are leveraging their large online following to host Twitter Spaces on various hot topics. To understand the current mediascape, it is imperative to contextualize it within Ghana's silenced histories, paying attention to the way that a growth in literacy and the diffusions of technologies have contributed to the nature of the media landscape today. Throughout this chapter, I have drawn connections between structural factors such as electricity access, educational access, and literacy rates and the evolution of the citizenry's access to media at the local and national levels. These discussions help us understand further the structural marginalization of Northern Ghana within the national imaginary and set the tone for us to better grasp the geographical context of the nation.

3

Subalterns, Griots, and Media

• •

A yi bɔli a yuli n ti lunsi nyin di lahi sɔɣiri zama ni

In chapter 2, we learned about the history of literacy and media development in Northern Ghana foregrounded in the history of infrastructural development during and after colonization and in the country's current neocolonial reality. We also learned about the relationship between media, technology, and literacy in the region. To understand the relationship between contemporary media and traditional media, we need to pay close attention to the material reality and lived experience of communities in the Northern part of the country and how that has shaped media as we know it today. Perhaps, to be sure, we cannot discuss media developments without understanding the growth and evolution of other technologies in the region. Here, I deconstruct subalternity and postcoloniality within this sociocultural context, bringing attention to the multiple levels of subalternity that communities in the North are often subjected to. I argue here that postcoloniality and subalternity shape not just the everyday lives of Northerners but also their everyday interactions with media and how these interactions overlap with media and technological evolution in the region. Subalternity is therefore translocated and contextualized here to draw parallels and overlaps between what is described as traditional media and contemporary media as we know it today.

Discussions of postcoloniality often analyze colonization utilizing the nation-state as a unit of analysis. While this is helpful to comparatively explicate social conditions across nations, it is important to note the colonial legacy embedded in the nation-state as a unit of analysis that often collapses the complexities and nuances in communities with diverse cultural and linguistic backgrounds into singular narratives. The colonial partition of Africa that laid the foundation for the construction of the nation-state is often defied by social organization in these communities that transcend imagined borders. For example, despite the arbitrary lines drawn to differentiate Ghana from Burkina Faso, Côte d'Ivoire, and Togo, ethnic groups, with their geosocial organization, often disregard and disrupt these borders. There are Dagaaba in the Upper West Region of Ghana, just as there are Dagaaba in Burkina Faso. The Mossi, who are found in the Northern Region, have a significant sibling population in Burkina Faso. These manifestations of geosocial organizations that defy borders complicate and even interrogate the notion of diasporas. This means that members of these communities often have relations and family members across borders. This diversity therefore needs to be accounted for as we seek to understand media growth and evolution in these communities. My use of postcoloniality here accounts for not just the violence of colonization on Global South communities but also how this violence has been maintained and reproduced in the postcolony by local representatives of the colonizer who have mounted an elite capture of the state and often work in the favor of the elite class while issues affecting the masses are relegated to the back burner.

Before we delve into the discussion of subalternity in Ghana, I would like us to unpack postcoloniality and its relevance to the argument that I make here. While some scholars have critiqued postcoloniality in reductionist tones by focusing on the "post" in postcoloniality and arguing therefore that we do not live in a postcolonial reality, I utilize postcolonialism here to draw focus to postcoloniality rather as a "contestation of colonial domination and the legacies of colonialism" (Loomba, 2005, p. 16). What this definition of postcoloniality does is open pathways to centering the silenced and forgotten histories of subaltern communities within the nation-state. This silencing has been perpetuated by the elite of the postcolony who often are the custodians of the master narratives of the nation. These custodians of the master narratives of the nation are usually people from geocultural and ethnopolitical groups that had early access to Western education and therefore were equipped to document the history of the nation-state in literary terms, thereby shaping the trajectory of the nation in the education sector, legal sector, and political realm. Geocultural groups, who for various reasons had no access to these social capital boosting tools, were ultimately erased in this national knowledge-building and history-making process. The groups with this level of intellectual and political power were therefore availed with a blank slate to write, rewrite, and unwrite the histories of the nation from their perspectives and identity locations. That the elite class develop master narratives in the nation-making process means that groups that have historically been marginalized in various structural ways are often pushed to the margins in this process of nation making, which not only defines national identity but has a significant impact on other aspects of the nation-making process. These are the silenced and subalternized stories that I bring attention to in this book. Postcolonialism therefore presents the opportunity to demarginalize the erased histories of subaltern communities whose erasure has been propelled by infrastructural poverty that casts them as mere spectators of history making and knowledge building. In this chapter, we see a bridging of this gap by drawing connections between traditional and contemporary media and Western ways of knowing and Indigenous ways of knowing.

Northern Ghana has been marginalized since colonization, and this marginalization persists today in the gaping economic, educational, political, health care, and infrastructural divide between the North and the South. Northern Ghana here refers to the five regions of the North—the Northern Region, the North East Region, the Savannah Region, the Upper East Region, and the Upper West Region—that share a history of disenfranchisement pre- and post-independence. For decades, there were only three geocultural regions of the North—the Northern Region, the Upper West Region, and the Upper East Region. In 2018, under President Nana Addo's government, the Northern Region, the largest, was further split into the North East and the Savannah Regions. The North-South divide discussed earlier means that Ghana as a nation-state is complicit in the epistemic violence to which these communities have historically been subjected. This epistemicide manifests in the erasure of Northern ethnic groups in nation-building and history-making efforts in the country. This erasure means that the North is often banished and removed from cultural and national citizenship, which is often centered on Southern communities, especially the Akan ethnic group and the nation's capital Accra. The North is often caught in a double bind where it is either symbolically annihilated from the national memory and present or bastardized in scant representations of the region in media narratives through tropes such as the North as uncivilized, savage, barbaric, violent, and resistant to Western modernization. These tropes mirror the historical and present representations of Africa in Global North media and in academic scholarship often by Global North scholars. This violence and erasure in representation in media and beyond is a distraction from the real work of knowledge building that is happening across various communities in the region. This epistemic violence is the reason why until this book there didn't exist scholarship that specifically analyzed the political economy of media focusing mainly on the diverse geocultural communities of (Northern) Ghana. This book not only interrogates this epistemic violence but contributes to building on the scant literature on media processes in subaltern communities.

Subalternity as postulated by Spivak (1994) has given us the tools to understand the way that hegemonic structures marginalize certain communities. Although subalternity has been widely applied to the South Asian context, I take this notion, subject position, and analytical framework and contextualize it within Ghana, focusing on its utility for understanding ethnicity and geography and how these concepts structure the makeup of Ghana as a nation-state. When I speak of the subaltern here, I am referring to ethnic groups that have been systematically written out of not just the Ghanaian public sphere but culture making in the country. Here, I am thinking of ethnic groups like the Konkomba/Bikpakpaam, Gonja, Builsa, Dagaaba, Waala, Kotokoli, and Kusaasi, among many others.

In this book I specifically focus on the Dagbamba, bringing attention to how their subalternity shapes the way that they are lumped together with other ethnic groups in the region and framed as Northerners in national media representations. As discussed in the introduction, my use of the referent "Dagbamba" focuses heavily on the Dagbanli-speaking community in the Northern Region. While my findings can be extrapolated to understand the experiences of the Mamprusi and Nanumba, who are close siblings of Dagbanli speakers, my interlocutors were mostly sampled from the Dagbaŋ community. While the concept "Northerners" can be useful in understanding ethnic groups in the region, their shared histories, and their proximity in culture and sometimes language, this referent often does not account for the diversity of and nuances embedded in the sociocultural constructions and realities of these groups. I use "Northerners" throughout the book to articulate the collective subalternity of ethnic groups in the North within the national context while also being cognizant of the complexities of the levels of marginality these groups occupy. For example, the Mole-Dagbamba are one of the largest ethnic groups not just in the Northern part of Ghana but also in the nation. They can thus be described as occupying a hegemonic position when it comes to population and cultural dominance in the North. This dominance means that Dagbamba can exert power over ethnic groups with smaller populations. The establishment of Radio Savannah in 1996 solidified this dominance by mediating content in Dagbanli and Gonja, while languages like Likpakpaln, Basare, Kotokoli, Bimoba, which are spoken by ethnic groups in the region, were further marginalized. Therefore, the Basare and the Bimoba are not just symbolically annihilated in national media representations but erased in regional media representations by state broadcasters such as the Ghana Broadcasting Corporation's Radio Savannah and other private commercial media organizations. However, collectively Dagbamba are systemically marginalized because of their late arrival to participating in Western educational structures due to British colonial resistance to establishing schools in the then–Northern Territories. According to lawyer Ibrahim Mahama, "The diabolical administrative and educational policies of the British in the Northern Territories put the people about a hundred years behind their compatriots in the Gold Coast" (2009, p. 114) Later, some Northern ethnic groups that embraced Christianity early were able to attend Christian mission schools as the educational space steadily opened up in the region. These established mission schools promoted and imposed Christian values on students irrespective of their religion. It is likely therefore that some Northern Christians who had early access to Western education may have had a leg up and may likely occupy important leadership positions in civil society and the political sphere today. The complexities and nuances in subalternity discussed here ultimately point to the permeability of subalternity and how it can evolve over time.

Indigenous Media in Traditional Society

Scholarly research on media in Africa often focuses on contemporary media such as TV, film, radio, the newspaper, and the internet. Research on Indigenous traditional media in many African communities often divorces it from contemporary media. This dissociation from contemporary media means that on some level media are decontextualized from the society within which they are situated, causing us to lose knowledge and epistemologies that connect all these forms of media. Existing literature that connects Indigenous media and knowledge systems to what is called contemporary media has examined it from the perspective of American scholar Paul Stoller (1992), who presents French anthropologist Jean Rouch as a cinematic griot due to his work in Niger that documents the lives of Nigeriens. This comparison of Rouch to griots in the West African tradition centers a white French man in the knowledge traditions of African communities. This limited analysis on the connection between Indigenous media and contemporary media (in)advertently decenters Africans as subjects in the process of history making.

Here, I am concerned with problematizing the notion of contemporary media and the ways in which it is presented in opposition to Indigenous media forms. I assert that all media forms that are part of society in the present are contemporary media. Therefore, drum music, drum chant (*salma*), *gonje* music, and others that are part of the current cultural landscape through naming ceremonies, marriage ceremonies, funerals, and festivals in many communities across Northern Ghana are contemporary media. I use the referent "Indigenous media" here to differentiate them from other mediums like TV, film, and radio. The drum is an important instrument in the lives of Dagbamba. Drums are not only used to make music for various dances such as *baamaya*, *takai*, and *tora* but also used in praise music (*salma*) and recounting the history and lineage of members of the community (Yamusah, 2013). According to MacGaffey (2013, p. 36), "Drum chant, or praise-singing (salima), a form of epic poetry, together with the complex repertoire of rhythms and dances and the ceremonies of chieftaincy, is the primary art form, closely associated with Dagbamba identity." Beyond the drum, the gonje is a musical instrument that is also used among the Dagbamba on various occasions and mainly for praise music. Like the drum, the gonje is an integral part of the cultural life of various communities across West Africa. The gonje, which has various names across these communities, is used by the Hausa and Yoruba people in Nigeria, the Songhai, Mauri, and Djerma in Niger, and the Mamprusi and Dagbamba in Ghana (Gourlay, 2001). Different variations of the gonje are used by ethnic groups in Senegal, the Gambia, Chad, and Burkina Faso.

Although many West African communities have a vibrant griot culture, there are nuances and complexities to these cultures, and they vary from community to community. Among the Dagbamba, the work of the griot is usually accompanied by drum music. The *lunsi* are among the most popular griots in this community. Lunsi is the plural of *luŋa*, which literally means "drum." Luŋa also means "drummer." But when luŋa is used to refer to a person, it does not mean just drummer since the concept takes on a more expansive definition. Luŋa therefore signifies musician, custodian of the culture, historian, entertainer, and teacher. It is not uncommon to find lunsi at naming ceremonies, marriage ceremonies, and funerals, where they present complex accounts of the lineages of community members. (See figure 1.)

And on special occasions, such as the Eid festival or the enskinment of a new chief, the *sambanluŋa* is assembled where lunsi recount the history of Dagbaŋ, making it relevant to the lineage of the chief in whose palace the sambanluŋa is assembled. Scholars have found that the role of the luŋa parallels that of the griot (MacGaffey, 2013; Ouattara, 2018). According to Issiaka Ouattara (2018, p. 154), "In African society, the griot is historian, storyteller, chronicler, musician, and so on. He is above all else the keeper of the art of speaking well and of speaking truth." Oratory becomes one of the most important skills of the griot and defines their competence. All of the responsibilities attributed to the griot are burdened not just on the individual griot but on griots as a collective who serve as custodians of history and culture. Therefore, although one is born into a luŋa family, one has to work toward becoming a luŋa by learning at the feet of elder lunsi. According to Abdul-Razak Wumpini (Luŋ Zaaku), a luŋa who appears on Sagani TV's cultural education program *Kavini*, younger lunsi practice *luntali* by playing at low-stakes events like market days to sharpen their griot and drum-playing skills (personal communication, March 15, 2023). In addition, patriarchal accounts of luntali via academic literature have focused on men lunsi while invisibilizing the labor and identities of women lunsi. This

FIGURE 1 Dagbaŋ *lunsi* at work. (Photo by Wunpini Fatimata Mohammed, 2023.)

phenomenon is ironic given that the luŋa is considered the "wife" of the chief due to their role as royal praise singers, historians, custodians of the culture, and so on. The close relationship of the lunsi to Dagbaŋ royalty demonstrates that the history of the kingdom becomes synonymous with the history of the exploits of the royals of the kingdom. Therefore, much like in other societies where history is written about powerful members of the community, Dagbaŋ history becomes the history of the royal families. This means that although griot culture can be useful for historicizing a community, it can reproduce the erasure of marginalized people in the community like commoners, women, and others.

In my conversation with Luŋ Zaaku, I learned that although *luŋ paɣaba* (women lunsi) are largely erased from popular narratives on luntali, they play a crucial role in the education and training of lunsi. Therefore, there is the general consensus that *luŋ paɣaba bihi* (the children of women lunsi) are more steeped in the luŋa tradition and are often very highly educated on the cultures and traditions of Dagbaŋ compared to *luŋ dabba bihi* (the children of men lunsi). Ultimately, whether one's luntali is acquired matrilineally or patrilineally determines the kind of luŋa one will become. In addition, although among the Dagbamba luŋ paɣaba do not typically drum, they sing praises and provide historical accounts at various important occasions. Some of them also sing Damba songs.

Ultimately, the epistemologies that have guided griot cultures in their myriad iterations are translocated by media makers such as filmmakers and radio

FIGURE 2 Dagbaŋ *gonje*. (Photo by Wunpini Fatimata Mohammed, 2023.)

journalists to produce media content that is not only relevant to their core audiences but also grounded in community values and knowledge systems. My discussion of the griot/luŋa/gonje here provides the context to understand the relationship between oral epistemologies and the political economy of media in Northern Ghana. (See figure 2.)

In this chapter, I highlight the connections between Indigenous media and other media like TV, film, and radio, demonstrating the ways in which they blur into and inform each other. There is a relationship between Indigenous knowledge systems and the work of griots, praise singers, Dagbanli journalists, and Dagbanli filmmakers. Throughout the chapter, I build on existing scholarly research and provide interventions to address the dearth of research drawing connections between Indigenous media and other media forms like TV, radio, and film. Praise singing and lineage tracking have been recorded and mediated on audio cassettes, videotapes, CDs, and more recently mobile phone camera and audio recording technology. The mediation of Indigenous epistemologies is just one aspect of the relationship between mediated mediums and Indigenous media. I demonstrate that there is a more nuanced relationship between orality and newer media forms like film and radio beyond the mediation of folklore, folktales, proverbs, and Indigenous music on these media platforms. My argument is set against the backdrop of my experiences as a community member engaging storytelling and the work of lunsi at various ceremonies. Participating in nighttime *simpa* dance events in Yendi and Tamale, listening to the mediation of Indigenous media on radio and watching it on TV, attending festivals like Damba and Buɣum, and learning from elders have positioned me strategically to theorize the rich knowledge making that occurs in these communities.

Subaltern Pedagogies, Community, and Media

Due to the historical marginalization of the region, the political economy of media has been affected by the structural factors that produce this marginalization. This means that media producers within this region often learn the trade through informal modes of education. This marginalization doubly affects Indigenous language media due to the lack of commitment to providing resources to promote literacy in Indigenous languages, as seen earlier. When I discuss informal circuits of education, I mean the circuits of education that do not follow the conventional Western model where individuals are specifically trained by educational institutions and equipped with the tools to do media production work in the area of news media journalism, filmmaking, videography, cinematography, and so on.

In this model, for example, Dagbanli news journalists learn hands-on from specific mentors in order to become fully trained as journalists. They begin as interns, learn from observing the work of mentors, and then learn by doing on their own. Others begin the learning process by observing (as audiences) the work of journalists they admire before taking the step of asking for formal guidance. This pedagogical strategy is not at all uncommon in other trades across the country, including dressmaking, hairdressing, and carpentry. People who learn these trades and professions are often trained for a couple of years until their "masters" decide that they are ready to be independent. Once this is determined, they graduate and start their careers within the trade. In the area of journalism, interns do grunt work such as learning the basics of writing a story, interviewing people, presenting the news, and producing a successful show among others. In this structure, there is not much of a difference between the English-language and Dagbanli-language newsroom; the difference here is in logistical support where although English newsrooms are not often equipped with the tools that they need to do their work, they are often better equipped than a Dagbanli or Gonja newsroom (Mohammed, 2019). This phenomenon may not necessarily apply to media organizations in other regions that exclusively transmit in an Indigenous language or mediums like digital television where some Tamale-based stations transmit almost exclusively in Dagbanli. While some in the English newsroom may be traditionally trained as journalists, the same cannot be said of Indigenous-language journalists. And when Indigenous-language journalists get any training, they practice as English-language journalists. Therefore, they often have to do additional work to become culturally competent to practice in the communities where they work. Beyond cultural competence, proficiency in the language of the community goes a long way to build relationships and trust with community members.

Beyond building trust and relatability with community members, it is important to understand that the strict divisions of commercial, public, and community media are often inadequate to understand the political economy of media in Ghana since these strict categorizations lose sight of the fact that the sociocultural context of these communities shapes how media are received and should be produced in these communities. For example, when Radio Tamale, a private commercial radio station, was established in 2016, the owners and managers decided that it would serve only the urban and cosmopolitan audience in Tamale and the Northern Region. They believed that there was a gap in radio programming for cosmopolitan audiences and thought that their station would better serve these communities. Their interpretation of this audience was narrowed to English-speaking middle-class audiences for whom hip and posh content would be produced. This decision was arrived at with no feasibility study to examine its commercial viability. Before long, the management of Radio Tamale realized that they not just failed to build a large audience community but also failed to raise revenue through advertising since it mostly came from adverts that targeted Dagbanli speakers. Once they realized that their urban radio model was going to flop, they quickly switched to a hybrid model in radio programming, like many other radio stations in the region, focused on both English and Dagbanli audiences. Also, most media audiences in the region are likely to be fluent in an Indigenous language. This assertion is supported by data from the country's 2021 population and housing census, which identifies the Northern Region as the largest illiterate population in the country (Ghana Statistical Service, 2022b). The census data also demonstrate that there are low levels of educational attainment in the region due to the earlier discussed structural factors. Widening the audience net to include Dagbanli-speaking audiences significantly improved the audience base of the media organization. In addition, due to the structural factors previously outlined, businesses often prefer to advertise their goods and services in the languages that their potential patrons speak. Therefore, the urban radio model not only made little commercial sense but also was exclusionary of large swaths of community members who are often excluded from national media representations. Ultimately, the categorizations of media organizations as commercial, public, and community need to be contextualized within the communities of operation. And this contextualization should account for the values of the community and what the community hopes to get out of media.

In the Tamale metropolis and in many other cities in the country, for example, audience participation is the bedrock of the mediascape where audiences phone in to programs like the morning show and other talk shows that focus on politics, health, agriculture, social relationships, and other topics. Although existing literature has often associated this attribute with community radio stations (Tsarwe, 2014), for example, commercial and public media have to incorporate this element in media programming to meet the needs of their audiences. Since the evolution of mobile phone technology, participation has been widened beyond phone in segments to include messaging through WhatsApp and other participatory modes on social media platforms such as Facebook and Twitter. In our attempts to understand media processes in the region specifically and the country as a whole, it is imperative to be cognizant of the role of communal participation in media processes and how media organizations can actively facilitate this to promote civic engagement and education. In this model therefore, the agency of audience communities is centered and the conditions are created for them to be empowered to utilize the media tools available to them to address issues affecting them. It is unsurprising therefore that one of the leading media programs in Northern Ghana is the Social Change Communication program at the University for Development Studies, Tamale, which is guided by the tenets of development communication.

Beyond participation in discussions on radio programs specifically, community participation has also manifested in a pedagogical manner where community members can phone in to correct the mistakes of panelists and radio hosts. Some of my memories of early radio in the Northern Region with the establishment of Radio Savannah in the late 1990s and early 2000s are speckled with instances of elderly community members, some of whom may have been custodians of the culture calling in to programs to make interventions about linguistic mispronunciations and inaccuracies and cultural imprecisions. When the stakeholder role of audience communities is built and strengthened, they are empowered to participate in the media production processes in ways that are shaped by their own experiences of collective knowledge-building models in their communities. Based on audience interest, other media organizations have taken community participation a step further by bringing in custodians of culture to provide cultural education about folklore, chieftaincy institutions, Dagbaŋ gastronomy, and so on. This type of education has not been limited to radio stations but has also seen an uptick in the programming of television stations. In the area of folklore, for example, some radio stations translocated *salma* (storytelling/folktales) to the radio realm to support the cultural education of children who may not necessarily have access to them. Salma means storytelling and also means drum chants/praise-singing. More recently television stations such as Sagani TV and Zaa TV have developed programs including *Kavini* and *Baŋsim Chuɣu*, respectively, to provide cultural education to Dagbanli audiences. In addition, the growth of digital TV means that audiences have a wide array of program choices to select from to gratify their media needs. This is a significant change from a media landscape where audiences were limited to programming from GBC's Ghana Television and Radio Savannah. Despite the wide interest in these development communication and cultural education initiatives, there is still little support from the government, civil society organizations, and nongovernmental organizations to support the self-determination of community members in this way. Recent efforts to revamp the work of the National Commission for Civic Education can work toward decentralizing civic education and expanding it to capture the interests of community members.

Indigenous Epistemologies, Pedagogy, and Radio

In earlier chapters, my discussion of Indigenous African knowledge systems brought attention to the hierarchies of knowledge and how Global South knowledge systems are often denigrated in favor of the canon that translates as Western ways of knowing. Although media studies is a relatively new discipline that grew up with the printing press, radio, and television, discussions about media studies within the African context have often sought to contextualize media within specific African communities. Despite efforts at building a body of knowledge on media on the continent and a growth in institutions that train media professionals, pedagogy has often leaned heavily on the Western curriculum (Mohammed, 2022b) with lecturers providing theoretical and practical skills to students to prepare them for industry. A decolonial approach to understanding media theory, pedagogy, and practice requires us to pay attention to the areas of media that are often erased or silenced in epistemology and praxis. Even though there is growing scholarship on the political economy of print, radio, TV, and digital media in many African countries, there is room for more work to be done to examine not just the intricacies of Indigenous-language media but the way that social and cultural organization and knowledge systems overlap with these media processes. I am interested in interrogating the relationship between African ways of knowing and media practices. I argue here that what we regard as traditional media (folklore, gonje, folktales, and other oral epistemologies) and contemporary media (TV, radio, digital media, etc.) blur into each other to produce content that not only is relevant to audiences but mirrors their everyday lives. Although traditional media processes have tremendously shaped media such as television, film, and radio, there is still a dearth of scholarship that draws these connections and creates pathways for us to better understand these overlaps. Some of these overlaps were born out of necessity due to infrastructural poverty, and others came about as a result of a natural evolution and growth of media within this sociocultural context.

In the early 1990s, there were efforts to promote functional literacy in Indigenous languages among community members in the Northern Region. Some of these programs, led by NGOs like School for Life, promoted literacy in Dagbanli and Likpakpaln so that communities in the region could be empowered to assert their agency. During this time, materials such as history books, textbooks, workbooks, and even storybooks were made available to promote African-language literacy. The late Zoosali Lana, Naa Tia Sulemana, not only was a staunch advocate of Dagbanli literacy but contributed to Dagbaŋ knowledge building by writing history books such as *Naa Luro mini o Bihi* (1970), which tracked the lineage and rule of Naa Luro. Works such as this not only contributed to knowledge building but supported the growth of written Dagbanli.

Media organizations have not had the logistical and funding support they need to grow Indigenous-language programming. This lack of logistical support in part has created what I call journalistic griots who reimagine the newsroom and the work of the journalist in very innovative ways (Mohammed, 2019). In 2017, I investigated the work of Gonja- and Dagbanli-language journalists and found that many of these journalists drew heavily on griot culture to support news production and presentation. I learned later that we do not have a physical Dagbanli keyboard or a keyboard in the Mabia languages of the North (which share a similar alphabet). The existing keyboard is a digital one, which means that the process of literary work in African languages can be tedious. This again draws attention to how the colonial hierarchization of languages starves African languages of literary growth (linguifam) and can lead to linguicide.

Due to limited access to, for example, Dagbanli keyboards to write and print news stories, these journalists who were often self-taught and benefited tremendously from the apprenticeship model discussed earlier became griots who presented news in Indigenous languages while looking through an English script ultimately turning framing theory and agenda-setting theory on its head (Mohammed, 2019).

Many of the journalists I spoke to lamented the lack of training programs in Dagbanli and Gonja at the various journalism educational institutions in the country. Some shared that they were perpetually in learning mode since they spent time among elderly members of the community and in spaces such as chief palaces to stay updated and proficient in the formal modes of these languages.

I called them journalistic griots because some of them compared their level of linguistic proficiency to that of griots (lunsi) who trained for years and had superior oratorical abilities as part of their professional duties. Here, we see a blurring of the praxis of lunsi (griots) and news presenters, demonstrating that these two media forms are not that different. A similar finding was observed in the Dagbanli film industry, which I discuss further in the next section.

Orality, Griot Culture, and Filmmaking

Media theorizing in Africa has not yet built a strong body of literature around certain subaltern media cultures and the ways in which they not only contribute to national media cultures but also interrogate ontology and conventional epistemologies around media political economy. This means that we are left with very little knowledge about how some marginalized communities assert their self-determination and self-actualization in the making, unmaking, and remaking of culture in various African communities. Here, we learn about what these intricacies look like in the silenced stories around media in Ghana. In my interactions with journalists, filmmakers, TV show hosts, media audiences, and other community members, I have found that much like other global geopolitical contexts, media in Northern Ghana shapes and mirrors society and societal values, and these mores in turn shape media in the processes of production, distribution, and reception. As we saw earlier, the communal values of the people of the region construct audiences not as passive consumers of media but as active consumers of and participants in media knowledge building. This phenomenon opens ways to conceptualize audience members as key players in preserving culture and societal values. This can be extrapolated to examine the extent to which community members and opinion leaders can be collaborators in the fight against disinformation and misinformation on digital platforms like WhatsApp, Facebook, and Twitter and sometimes on legacy media such as radio and television. Therefore, the extent of community participation is not a dividend of democracy but rather a product of the social construction in the community that emphasizes community-driven knowledge production, community accountability praxes, communal care around knowledge making, and community-informed strategies that constitute the core of the media political economy in this region.

Before I delve into unpacking the relationship between oral epistemologies and filmmaking, I share another example of how a community accountability praxis was deployed to challenge a gross misrepresentation of Dagbaŋ culture on-screen. In December 2021, a film titled *Savannah* (Kobi Rana, 2021) premiered at the Silverbird Cinemas in Accra. The film interrogates patriarchal systems by throwing light on the harms that the practice of female genital mutilation does to girls. The narrative of the film was focused on the culture and language of Dagbamba who have never practiced or supported female genital mutilation. Leading up to the premiere, Dagbon Forum, a group organized around the development and growth of Dagbamba, drew attention to the misrepresentation of the cultures of this ethnic group and the lasting negative impact this film would have on the community. A member of Dagbon Forum and sociologist, Dr. Alhassan Sulemana Anamzoya, wrote a letter to the minister of tourism, arts, and culture to protest this representation of the Dagbaŋ Kingdom. In the letter, titled "Dagbon Would Not Sit Down for the World to Be Misinformed by Venus Films Production," Dr. Anamzoya argued that the use of Dagbanli and the architectural space of the region linked the kingdom to a practice that it has never been known to participate in or endorse. This letter caught the attention of community members who organized on Facebook and Twitter to protest the movie and call for its boycott. Other community members and stakeholders in the Dagbanli film industry in Tamale where there was to be a screening of the film worked to cancel the film's presentation in the region. Community and industry stakeholders met with producers of the film to hold them accountable and educate them on the harms of such misrepresentations. Although the producers apologized and expressed remorse, the film was still screened in Accra. The concerns raised by the community made sense since Northern Ghanaian cultures have often been stereotyped as barbarous by mainstream media and these representations have colored the lived experience of Northerners across the country and in the African diaspora. The involvement of the community in this type of media activism highlights the importance of utilizing subaltern theories to understand media political economy in the global context. This example is illustrative of the ways in which media audiences assert their agency to actualize their self-determination.

Beyond community-driven media activism, other media processes such as filmmaking need to be understood and theorized within the context of Indigenous knowledge systems. Here, I bring our attention back to a locally grown regional film industry that tremendously shaped pop culture and the entertainment industry of the Northern Region. I demonstrate here the ways in which Indigenous knowledge systems constitute an integral part of knowledge making in the movie industry. My intent here is to illustrate what collectively produced knowledge in the film industry looks like and the ways in which it draws from community values around epistemology even in the entertainment industry. Interlocutors in the Dagbanli movie industry often employ innovative strategies inspired by community ways of being in film production by working with the intellectual and logistical tools available to them. What I call the "oral film script," which I discuss at length, is a product of a sociocultural context that has been shaped by the various structural factors that have influenced literacy, education, and technological development.

Script writing is an integral part of the filmmaking process not only because a script breaks down the dialogue of the film but also because it is a place where the imagination of what the film will look like is brought to life in words. Just like many Dagbanli radio journalists who are not taught traditional journalism in educational institutions, many Dagbanli filmmakers learn through the apprenticeship model or through self-teaching. This means that filmmakers and actors pull from their everyday experiences and observations and communal knowledge to bring films to life. For most film industries, the script is the crux of any film production. In the Dagbanli film industry, however, the script manifests unconventionally in what I call the "oral script." In the next chapter, we will learn about the way that filmmakers in the industry grow and develop their artistic skills over time on the job. Since many filmmakers are self-taught, very few are knowledgeable about the intricacies of conventional script writing and production. Therefore, filmmakers here have come up with innovative ways to produce scripts. This style of script production goes hand in hand with the culture of weekly rehearsals at drama group meetings where actors rehearse plots usually developed by the leader of the group. This mode of rehearsal helps actors to develop characters across various roles and facilitates their work on location when they are cast for roles.

The oral film script was the most common form of script that was used by many filmmakers in the industry. The filmmaker or director usually has this script in their memory and narrates to actors at rehearsals or on location and asks them to take on the personality of the characters presented. While the cinematic griot concept (Fisher, 2016; Smith, 2010; Tomaselli and Sakarombe, 2015) was developed to understand how filmmakers incorporated orature and orality in the content of films, I expand this concept further. Here, the cinematic griot not only translocates orality to the screen but also embodies the characteristics of the griot where they commit scripts to memory and direct films from the oral scripts they have in memory. These actors and filmmakers extend their griot skills to their drama groups where they transmit knowledge they learned from pioneering filmmakers or as pioneering filmmakers to young artists in the industry. They become cinematic griots on location as artists in the film industry and at weekly drama group meetings where they impart knowledge to emerging artists. Therefore, this regional film industry disrupts the Western construction of filmmaker as director and reconfigures the notion of filmmaking as a collaborative process between the director and actors to bring a story to life. Within this context, actors who are coproducers and collaborators on film production embody the characteristics of the cinematic griot. A director shares his creative process that illustrates the oral film script: "Everyone knew me for my directing skills. I didn't write scripts for films. Everything was in my head. I would direct films from beginning to end without looking at a script. And this is how I've taught people like Sherifatu Issah and others. When Sherifa directs a movie, she does not look at a script and she does the directing perfectly" (Alhassan Iddrisu Dawuni aka Afa Digital, personal communication, 2018). Similarly, this filmmaker recounts how she directs actors to embody a character in a film:

> Like I said, when I build the script in my head, I begin to figure out who I want to cast and how I want the story represented. If someone was framed for a crime and they have to seek justice at the chief's palace you have to think about what the chief will say, what the accused will say because you cannot call a chief a liar. How do you defend yourself in front of the chief who believes the lie that was told against you? You have to figure it out . . . the dialogue and the ways in which you speak respectfully to the chief. You have to be respectful when you speak to the chief even when you are disagreeing with him. (Sherifatu Issah, personal communication, 2018)

Here, Sherifatu Issah discusses her artistic process as a filmmaker, making sure to ground it in the linguistic conventions of the community within which the narrative is set. Although her work is not guided by a traditional script, there are certain parameters within which she operates that work to reflect not just the lived reality of the community but also conversational conventions within the socially situated context. For example, the language used to address a chief is different from that used to address any other community member because the language conventions require linguistic deference in the presence of the chief. While a few filmmakers worked on what they called a written English narrative script, the oral script used in Indigenous-language films that was presented verbally was widely popular in the industry. With the written English narrative script, the director summarized the plot of the film and used it to guide their directing of the film. These narrative scripts almost never had dialogues since directors believed that it was not needed because the actualization of the script was done in Dagbanli by actors who were conversant with and had practiced in this industry tradition. Other filmmakers revealed that having a written English script defeated the entire purpose of directing since most of the actors were neither literate nor proficient in English to read the script in preparation for their roles: "Most of [the actors] cannot read so my studio manager actually did the translation for them which they rehearsed. Most of the dialogues where we really wanted the person to say just as we had written it, we rehearsed it with them. We knew they couldn't read. We had to make sure that what we had written was properly translated into Dagbanli and the way they say it should be the typical Dagbanli not the diffused one" (Leonard Kubaloe aka OBL, personal communication 2018). Filmmakers like Leonard Kubaloe, who worked on the conventional script, still had to work with actors to bring the dialogue to life in Dagbanli, and people proficient in Dagbanli were consulted to ensure linguistic accuracy and depth in these translations. Therefore, although the final product of films represented Dagbanli, it was rare to find a filmmaker working with a Dagbanli film script due to limited levels of literacy in Dagbanli on the part of both actors and filmmakers. Therefore, a lack of literacy in English and Dagbanli did not deter artists (actors, producers, and filmmakers) from telling stories on the screen. Rather, these artists looked to Indigenous knowledges within the context of language proficiency and griot culture to enrich the narratives that were represented and curate them to more accurately reflect the linguistic culture and lived experience of this community. Here, filmmaker Alhassan Yushawu Jahanfo (personal communication, 2018) emphasizes how actors and some directors' limited literacy in English and Dagbanli forced them to find innovative ways to produce films: "It's only the director who will be having it [the script] in mind and will be giving the . . . but now people are writing even the dialogue. They will write it but because we are shooting in Dagbanli even if I give the dialogue, some of them cannot read so you will have to keep it to yourself and say it verbally to the actor. The person cannot read the Dagbanli even if you have it on paper, you just have to do away with that and then say it verbally."

Some filmmakers lamented the limitations that an oral script posed to the process of filmmaking. According to them, measures were put in place to present directors and filmmakers with the skills and knowledge in script writing, even if actors were not literate in English or Dagbanli: "It's not only standard script usage but you can't go to location without putting something on paper. At the workshop we are organizing, I think somebody will be there to guide our scriptwriters as to how to write the standard script. We do put down our stories on paper but the professional way of writing it is the problem. It wasn't like that at first, we will go to location and you ask of the script to go through and you can't find it" (personal communication, Alhassan Yushawu Jahanfo, 2018). Working with an oral script means that actors need to be highly proficient in Dagbanli to properly play their roles. Actors are usually expected to speak advanced Dagbanli, especially in films that are set in villages, to boost the linguistic authenticity of the film. Some filmmakers noted that actors were as much a part of the screenwriting process as directors and filmmakers since it was the actors who developed the dialogue for the roles they played while directors presented the narrative script and helped actors perfect the dialogue.

> God has given us something here. Our actors here, God has given them brains, sharp brains. When you write your script, bring them together and read the whole story from A to Z before you sit down and cast it. Because most of them can't read, you are going to be reading and then giving them the guidelines. So here our director has problems because every actor must know his role and dialogue because you are going to be giving them the dialogue and directing at the same time and the moment you start it. The moment you know the role. If I say you, you are going to be a queen and you are going to be harsh, the rest you know how you are going to do it. It's only the dialogue I will correct you. That is the talent God has given to our people here. The moment you tell them you are the king, the queen, they all know what to do. It's only the dialogue that you have read and the movement, so we don't have many problems with our actors on the location ground. (Hamidu Fuseini aka Nba Gomda, personal communication, 2018)

That actors contribute immensely to building the dialogue a character participates in demonstrates the collaborative process of filmmaking in this community. They specifically help bring the story to life, which makes the work of the director easier. Ultimately, both the directors and actors embody the role of the cinematic griot as in their respective roles they all play their part as griots to bring the oral script to life. Therefore, filmmaking in this context is a cultural performance in which directors and actors collaborate to bring the characters and story to life. Although a lack of literacy may have its limitations, the artists are right at home since they pull from already existing orature and orality within the knowledge systems of this community.

Language is important not just for communication but also because it is the vehicle through which culture is made, unmade, and remade; language is the vehicle for history making, and the death of a language means the death of a people and of the essence of a people. Communities whose knowledge systems are based in orality and oral epistemologies should not be pushed to the periphery. There is room for multiple ways of knowing to coexist and perhaps even complement each other. According to Ngũgĩ wa Thiong'o (1993, p. 19), "the importance of the oral tradition is that through its agency African languages in their most magical form have been kept alive. One of the highest developments of this was the *griot* tradition in West Africa. Whole epics and histories of families and nations were banked in the memories of these keepers of the word." Among Dagbamba this griot tradition has been carried on by the lunsi and the gonje who continue to be the custodians of history, culture, and the present narratives of the community. It is therefore not surprising that artists and creative workers such as actors, filmmakers, musicians, and journalists have drawn extensively on these knowledge traditions to enrich their work and to more accurately mirror society. Here, there isn't a clear-cut line between traditional media (praise singing, folklore, proverbs, etc.) and other media such as TV, radio, and film; there is a marriage between these types of media and the knowledge that produces them. This type of hybridity is reminiscent of the marriage of cultures in the pre-internet and pre-legacy media age. Although certain knowledge systems are still elevated above others (wa Thiong'o, 2012), the phenomenon of hybridity discussed here demonstrates the malleability of culture while drawing attention to how cultural resilience can evolve in our current media reality.

Centering Subalternity in Knowledge Making

As we center subaltern ways of being and knowing in our quest to better understand the political economy of media in the Global South and how it interconnects with indigeneity, it is imperative to note the threat that the globalization of neoliberalist values and ways of engagement with Global South communities poses to the growth of southern knowledges. There is room for various ways of knowing to coexist, and given that the Global South makes up majority of the world, it is important to begin examining the alternative ontologies and epistemologies that have always existed in Indigenous communities that have been structurally marginalized due to colonialism and imperialism. Centering subalternity is important to understanding the ways in which the globalization of dominant media from the Global North (read: Hollywood) can serve as a threat to knowledge making in Africa and other Global South regions. As corporate multiculturalism couched as globalization seeks to co-opt and commodify local and Indigenous knowledge for the Western gaze, the needs of African audiences become secondary while the commercial imperatives shaped by ratings and views are pursued. Again, there is hope in learning from global Indigenous values that are centered around community, sustainability, and accountability to undo the reproduction of power hierarchies not just in what stories get told but in who tells these stories and what values underpin these tellings.

4

African Cinemas, Globalization, and Resistance

● ●

O di mali mali; Baya bila di mali mali ti paai tuɔm

In Northern Ghana, the early memory of drama points to Dagbanli video films and early radio dramas like *Baatoro*, which was widely patronized by the community. While the Dagbanli movie industry began in the late 1980s, Dagbanli radio dramas on GBC's Tamale-based Radio Savannah were broadcast in the late 1990s. *Baatoro* was arguably the most popular show on Radio Savannah and was patronized by young and old people alike. In the late 1990s, Sundays came to be established as special days for listening to this radio soap opera that explored various social topics. Some of the popular themes focused on topics such as marriage, polygyny, and romantic and familial relationships. During the holy month of Ramadan, themes about how to be a good Muslim, how to properly observe the thirty-day fast, and Ramadan-related comedy were explored. These themes were relevant to the community since Northern Ghana has the largest population of Muslims in the country. Ultimately, Dagbanli radio dramas and cinema came to coexist side by side with actors playing various roles in various productions on radio and in film. This is how the Dagbanli video film industry came to be sustained for decades. We saw earlier the way that media development in radio overlapped and intersected with technological growth and how this growth converged with the political economy of the movie industry. In this chapter, I unpack the history of the Dagbanli film industry to facilitate our understanding of its political economy in current times.

I argue that to understand how the Dagbanli movie industry has been sustained for over three decades, it is imperative to examine critically the industry's history and the innovative strategies filmmakers have employed to keep up with changing trends in technology and aesthetics in the industry. This chapter draws on and complements the oral histories and collective memories about the Dagbanli movie industry.

While there has been extensive research on anglophone and francophone cinemas in West Africa, little attention has been paid to Indigenous-language cinemas in the region. There has been some research on Nigeria's Hausa language Kannywood (Adamu, 2007; Larkin, 2008) but very little on Indigenous-language cinemas in Ghana. In this chapter, I draw attention to the dearth of research on Indigenous-language media in Ghana while providing an extensive history of Indigenous-language cinemas in the country.

Cultural Flows Within the Global South

In many African countries like Ghana, Nigeria, and Kenya, the British colonizers utilized film as a medium to promote colonial propaganda, for health instruction, and for other educational purposes (Smyth, 2013). During this time, the major aim of film was to "better" colonize and control the African subject. This strategy was more directly enforced in apartheid South Africa, where film was censored for African audiences; censorship included erasing images that promoted Black resistance of white supremacy and imperialism in the country (van Staden, 2017). Although the colonial government believed that film was an important avenue to communicate colonial policies to colonized subjects in Africa, it was not until 1948 that the continent's first film school was established in Accra, with another in Kenya opening the following year (Smyth, 2013).

Violent Hollywood westerns became popular with audiences for their thrilling content (Barlet, 2010; van Staden, 2017) in a range of locations including Ghana, Cameroon, and South Africa. According to van Staden (2017), westerns were popular in South Africa because Black South Africans consumed them to subvert and resist white supremacy and apartheid. Hong Kong kung fu films were popular in many African countries for their thrilling mise-en-scène and how affordable and accessible they were to the masses (Barlet, 2010; van Staden, 2017). Before long, Bollywood caught the attention of film audiences in Muslim communities in Nigeria, Egypt, Mali, Senegal, Benin, Cameroon, Togo, Guinea, Niger, and Morocco (Barlet, 2010) and across the continent for various reasons including cultural proximity (Adamu, 2010; Larkin, 2008) and the interest of the Indian diaspora (Virdi, 2017) living in African countries like South Africa, Mauritius, Kenya, and Tanzania.

More than anything, cultural proximity has been identified as the reason for the popularity of Bollywood films with African audiences. Many African audiences not only found Bollywood films entertaining with the songs and glamor depicted but found them to be relatable (Barlet, 2010). For Muslim northern Nigeria and other African communities, it is the closest audiences could get to representations of modesty and Islam (Adamu, 2010; Barlet, 2010). Hausa youth could identify with Indian films because of similarities in cultural items such as clothing. Bollywood film characters were usually dressed in "flowing saris, turbans, and head covers, especially in the earlier historical Hindi films shown in cinemas throughout northern Nigeria in the 1960s" (Adamu, 2010, p. 47). In recent times, Bollywood cinema has significantly waned in popularity with African audiences because the films have become increasingly Westernized (Barlet, 2010). African "female audiences are mad about Brazilian, Mexican or Peruvian soap operas such as *Sinners, Barbarita, Women of Sand, Lorenzo's Wife, Marimar, Muñeca Brava, Rubi, Family Ties*, etc." in the past decade (Barlet, 2010, p. 140). Later in this chapter, I map the historical connections in Global (South) cultural flows to the Dagbanli film industry, presenting their relevance to the history of and current trends in the industry.

The History of Film in Nigeria and Ghana

Ghana's and Nigeria's video film industries are both shaped by the culture and political climate of the respective countries. When the countries were British colonies, the Colonial Film Units in Ghana and Nigeria were utilized to further colonialist propaganda. In both countries, the need to produce films that reflected the lived reality of citizens was one of the major reasons for the advent of and growth of the film industries. In early Nigerian cinemas, the themes around which Nollywood video films revolved were "betrayal, infidelity, love, and revenge," while the most popular genres were "love, romance, history, folklore, witchcraft, juju, and drama" (Onuzulike, 2007, p. 25). Interestingly, similar themes and genres developed in the Ghanaian movie industry from the 1990s to the 2000s (Aveh, 2010).

From the colonial to the postcolonial era, the Ghanaian video film industry underwent several changes, some of which were necessitated by the political climate and limited state funding of the industry (Aveh, 2010; Garritano, 2013; Meyer, 2015). Many of the works produced in the Ghanaian and Nigerian movie industries are described as video films because movies were shot in "video form due to the high cost of celluloid" (Onuzulike, 2009, p. 176). As the industry grew with the influx of untrained filmmakers, it was not long before Nigerian video films began to flood into the industry, which some scholars attribute to the decline of the Ghanaian industry (Aveh, 2010). The early history of Indigenous-language Ghanaian cinemas can be traced to Egbert Adjesu's (1970)

English- and Akan-language movie *I Told You So*. However, it took some time before commercial filmmaking took off in the country. William Akuffo's *Zenabu* (1986) has been identified as the video film that ushered commercial filmmaking into the country (Aveh, 2010). Through conversations with interlocutors, I found that, much like Nollywood and Ghallywood, the Dagbanli movie industry was established to mediate the lived reality of communities in the Northern Region.

Existing scholarly work on film in Ghana focuses on the English-language video film industry Ghallywood, whose name has been under contention for years (Aveh, 2010; Garritano, 2013; Meyer, 2015), while little attention has been paid to the Indigenous-language movie industries across the country. When documenting the history of film in Ghana, it is imperative to note the intersections between film, TV, and radio in the country and how these intersections have shaped the growth of local movie industries. These intersections have been parsed out in chapter 2. The Ghana Broadcasting Corporation (GBC), via Ghana Television (GTV) and GBC radio, has done extensive work to bring movies and radio soap operas to local audiences, some of whom for various reasons would not have access to media like these. The growth in radio soap operas in the early 1990s also demonstrates radio's role in shaping the growth of not just drama but film. In conversations with pioneering filmmakers, I found that many stakeholders in the Dagbanli movie industry played a significant role in the growth of radio soap operas like *Baatoro* and TV shows like *Showcase in Dagbani*. It is imperative to note that in recent times there has been growth in Indigenous-language movie industries in the Upper West Region, the Volta Region, and elsewhere.

Despite the role that GBC and some commercial media platforms have played in the production of media content in Indigenous Ghanaian languages, very little attention has been paid to Indigenous-language media in African and Ghanaian media studies. My conversations with filmmakers in 2018 serve as a guide on our journey of learning the histories of film in Northern Ghana. This chapter maps the history of Indigenous-language film in Northern Ghana, making connections between this industry and other film industries in the country and elsewhere. The analysis here is filtered through my knowledge of and experiences with Indigenous African knowledge systems, which provide conceptual grounding to understand the political economy of media in Northern Ghana. "Indigenous knowledge specifically in many African communities is passed down from generation to generation and these types of knowledges are used and applied in various aspects of quotidian life that include language and literature, technology, education, healthcare, agriculture, environmental conservation, fashion, food and nutrition, etc." (Mohammed, 2019, p. 238). Bringing these sensibilities to understanding these histories, I demonstrate that filmmakers intentionally draw on Dagbaŋ culture and other localized knowledge systems to thematically and aesthetically enrich their movies. Therefore, to map the history of this Indigenous film industry, I weave the experiences and knowledge shared by filmmakers (from quotes via interviews) with my analysis of the industry to highlight the complexities of my interlocutors' role in contributing to the development of the political economy of media in Tamale and beyond.

Indigenous-Language Screen Media in Ghana

Here, I build on the context I provided earlier in the chapter about the history and complexities of cinema and television in Ghana. Filmmaking in Ghana has historically been associated with the English-language movie industry, Ghallywood. This industry produced movies in English, meaning that a large portion of the Ghanaian population had limited access to and interest in these movies. Indigenous-language audiences in the early 1990s however were treated to Indigenous-language content on television shows such as the *Showcase* series that presented TV programs in a few of the dominant Indigenous Ghanaian languages. This TV show followed the same format but presented content in the various Ghanaian languages and attempted to explore themes that Indigenous audiences of these languages would find relevant. For example, dates were assigned to each series and the series were titled based on the language the content was in, such as *Showcase in Dagbani, Showcase in Ga, Showcase in Akan, Showcase in Ewe*, and so on. Apart from the *Showcase* series, the *Concert Party* series that constituted comedy staged for audiences and distributed on TV (in Akan) was widely popular, especially in Southern Ghana.

Many of the actors and producers in the *Showcase in Dagbani* series were instrumental to the growth of the Dagbanli video film industry in Northern Ghana. While they produced the showcase series for the consumption of Dagbanli audiences on national television, they continued to work toward building an already existing regional movie industry to supplement the content produced for TV audiences. In 1989, the first Dagbanli movie was produced to fill the gap in movie content in Indigenous Ghanaian languages. According to industry pioneers, this is the oldest Indigenous-language movie industry in the country in which multiple filmmakers and producers consistently produced movies. Before the Dagbanli video film industry was established, Bollywood films were popular with cinema audiences in Northern Ghana, especially the regional capital Tamale. Ultimately, Dagbanli movies fulfilled audiences' desire to see themselves represented on the screen in their own language.

Although the oldest Ghanaian movie industry, Ghallywood, has seen tremendous growth, the Indigenous-language movie industries like Kumawood and the Dagbanli movie industry have always been more popular with and more linguistically accessible to the masses because they often represent the lived reality and represent topics of interest to many Ghanaians especially in rural communities.

Indigenous-Language Cinemas from Kano to Tamale

Tamale and Kano are both northern cities in Ghana and Nigeria, respectively. The Dagbamba and the Hausa share historical connections through trade and religion. There is a Hausa Zango in Tamale where people of Hausa descent originally settled, though today it is inhabited by people of varying ethnicities including the Hausa. A Zango, in Ghana, is a settlement in urban areas that are specifically designated for people read as migrants (usually predominantly Muslim) from various communities across Ghana, Nigeria, Burkina Faso and other neighboring countries. The Hausa Zango in Tamale, which is traditionally governed by the Zango chief, is a place of convergence for the two ethnic groups. The first Dagbanli film, *ŋuni Taali*, was released in 1989; in 1990 the first Hausa-language film, *Turmin Danya*, was released in Kano, Nigeria (Adamu, 2007). The two cities share similarities in Islam (as the dominant religion) but are shaped by the dominant ethnic group—the Dagbamba for Tamale and the Hausa for Kano.

There was some Bollywood influence in media consumption in the Northern Region of Ghana in the 1990s. During this time cinema structures were put up where people paid to see Indian movies. Some of these theaters were inside compound houses with a single communal entrance; others were wooden or straw (*gbala*) buildings established for the sole purpose of screening (Bollywood) films. According to Larkin (2008), Indian films shaped popular culture in Northern Nigeria during this period; I found that around this time Indian films were popular in Northern Ghana too. The persistence of the existence of Indian cultural flows can be seen in recent times in Muslim Northern Ghanaian marriage ceremonies in which some brides who change into several elegant clothes have a specific outfit they change into known as "Indian wear." Therefore, Indian cinema and TV not only shaped popular culture in these regions but ultimately influenced the cultural imagination of the predominantly Muslim North. We learn more about Indian pop cultural and Bollywood influences in the Northern Ghanaian culture industries in chapter 5.

Although the Hausa of Northern Nigeria have an extensive documented literary tradition (Adamu, 2007; Larkin, 2008), the same cannot be said of the Dagbamba of Northern Ghana, who have relied heavily on oral epistemologies (Hale, 2007). Also, whereas Islam extensively shapes the cultural imaginary of Northern Nigeria, in the case of the Northern Region of Ghana ethnicity has shaped Islam in many ways. Here, I examine the similarities and differences between the two film industries, paying attention to the role of global cultural flows in these cinematic influences.

Unlike the Dagbamba, the Hausa who fully embraced Islam in the ninth century utilized the literary affordances that the Islamic language of Arabic presented not just to document the history of the ethnic group but to develop a literary tradition beyond the Islamic religion (Adamu, 2007). This evolution in literacy meant that the Hausa were able to document key moments in their history well ahead of many other ethnic groups in Nigeria (Adamu, 2007). It is believed that this literary tradition has existed for over five hundred years (Adamu, 2007). Islamic influences among the Dagbamba can be traced to the reign of Naa Zanjina in the eighteenth century (Hamid, 2010). Today, Islamic influences manifest in various festivals like Damba and Buɣum celebrated by the Dagbamba. These influences pervade other cultural traditions and rituals in childbirth (naming), marriage, and death. This book opens ways of learning about the Ajami script literary tradition in the Northern Region and the extent to which it shaped media evolution (if at all) and what has become of it today.

One of the major issues that many postcolonial African nations grapple with is ethnic representation in national media. In many African countries and elsewhere, intellectually dominant and politically powerful ethnic groups often have structural power and tend to dictate what the mediascape looks like as far as linguistic content is concerned. In Ansah's (1986) discussion of the evolution of radio in Ghana, he examines what ethnic and linguistic pluralism means for Ghana as many ethnic groups are usually left out of programming due to the large number of Indigenous languages in the country. Therefore, linguistically, politically, and intellectually dominant ethnic groups tend to overshadow the *others* in (regional and national) media representation. Therefore, while Dagbanli is marginalized in media representations at the national level, it dominates media representation at the regional level on platforms such as radio, contemporary music, and satellite television. Likpakpaln (spoken by the Konkombas/Bikpakpaam), on the other hand, has historically been marginalized at the national and regional levels as far as media representation is concerned.

Just as Pentecostal Christianity dominates religious content on legacy media with nationwide coverage in Ghana, Muslim communities in Nigeria are marginalized in religious mediation in the South (Ihejirika, 2009). Muslim Nigeria's similarity to Muslim Ghana points to the cultural proximity of the Hausa and Dagbamba and provides justification for theorizing the Dagbanli film industry, paying attention to work that has already been done on Kannywood. Building an argument on this cultural proximity does not necessarily mean that the nuances in this industry will be overlooked for blatant similarities and differences with Kannywood. Rather, scholarly work on Kannywood serves as a backdrop for understanding the evolution of Kannywood to produce work that can be useful for future research on both the Dagbanli and Hausa film industries.

Like I question the dearth of literature in Northern Ghanaian film, Larkin (2008) questions the seeming lack of scholarly interest in the intercultural relationship between Bollywood and Kannywood. There has since been a steady growth in research on the Northern Nigerian Kannywood movie industry. While there has been extensive artistic collaboration between Nollywood and Ghallywood (English-language cinemas), my research demonstrates that there has been no contact between Kannywood movie producers in Northern Nigeria and the Dagbanli movie industry.

A History of Dagbanli Movies

Before the establishment of the Dagbanli movie industry, Bollywood romance musicals, American action war films, and Chinese films were popular in Northern Ghana. These films were usually screened at the two cinemas in Tamale, Victory and Rivoli. Bollywood films were usually screened at noon and at eight o'clock in the evening and were quite popular with youthful audiences especially young (married) women. Later, these films were screened at video centers in various suburbs of the city and in rural areas across the region. But it was not until the late 1980s that audiences began to see movies in their own languages. I draw from conversations with pioneering filmmakers to present a history of Dagbanli video films in Northern Ghana and how the industry has evolved over time.

The first Dagbanli movie, ŋuni Taali (Whose fault?), which was directed by Abubakari Sadiq and released in 1989, focused on themes such as family, relationships, and household issues. Subsequent movies like Naabaala (Abdul Rahman Amangai, 1992), Ya Nmaha (Nowhere cool; Alhaji Rashid Bawa BBC, 1990) explored similar themes. According to a pioneering actor and filmmaker of the Dagbanli video film industry, Alhaji Rashid Bawa (popularly known as BBC), ŋuni Taali was released on June 10, 1989. He revealed that the first meeting of key players and stakeholders in the production and making of the movie was held on February 18, 1989. Bawa shares a synopsis of the movie: "The first script was a script based on social issues and it was called ŋuni Taali. That was the first movie, [the title means] Whose Fault? The film was about a young girl who was abandoned by the father and actually went into prostitution. She got pregnant so she wanted to abort it and unfortunately, she died. So they wanted to know whose fault it was. Was it the girl's fault? Was it the mother's fault? Was it the father's fault? And I actually played the doctor in that movie" (personal communication, Alhaji Rashid Bawa aka BBC, 2018).

The topics explored in this first movie draw attention to the roots of social change communication in the Northern media landscape, a phenomenon we explored in chapter 2. The first Dagbanli movie was produced because the pioneers saw an opportunity in the relative absence of cinematic and theatrical art production in the North compared to the South. They observed that staged dramas had become popularized by the Akan-language Obra Drama Group and therefore decided that it was time for them to contribute to Dagbanli representation on the stage and in the cinema. The pioneers took things a step further in addressing this gap by bringing art to the cinema through Dagbanli movies. Therefore, the Dagbanli video film industry is the oldest Indigenous-language video film industry in Ghana since, according to industry stakeholders, it existed for years before Kumawood officially took off.

While GBC worked to present Indigenous-language media content through programs such as the *Showcase* series, there remained scant representation in film content in Dagbanli and several Northern Ghanaian languages. As mentioned earlier, the *Showcase* series, widely popular in the 1990s, brought Indigenous-language television content to viewers across the country. While the artists had creative control over the thematic and aesthetic aspects of these TV shows, they had little control over distribution since it was managed by GBC, which commissioned these projects.

According to industry pioneers Alhaji Rashid Bawa (BBC) and Hamidu Fuseini (Nba Gomda), the Biehisuŋ Drama Group was the first drama group to be established in the movie industry. Since the first Dagbanli movie release resulted in the creation of the Biehisuŋ Drama Group, drama groups have become an integral part of the industry and most movie productions are organized around the work of members of these groups. The early Dagbanli movie industry was kept alive by drama groups like Biehisuŋ Drama Group, Alaafee Drama Group, Simli Drama Group, Suhuyini Drama Group, and Suɣlo Drama Group. Many of these drama groups went on to stage radio dramas on *Baatoro* (in the early 2000s) after the local state broadcaster Radio Savannah was established in 1996.

In the 2020s, the Dagbanli movie industry still produces movies through drama groups that are known as "mother groups," which meet weekly for rehearsals and conduct other industry business. Mother groups are usually the primary drama groups of which actors, producers, and directors are members. Mother groups are a common phenomenon in the industry where group members meet weekly to rehearse for movies, support the careers of various members, and pay dues to sustain the group. These mother groups are organized under one umbrella known as the Northern Drama and Filmmakers Association (NORDRAFIM), which met every Sunday as of the time of ethnographic observation in 2018.

In the late 1980s and early 1990s, analog technology was used to shoot, edit, and produce Dagbanli movies. While a few camera operators had some training in operating cameras, like Zakaria Abdullai (Zakvilla) from his workplace at the Information Services Department, many camera operators and technicians were self-taught. Analog cameras were used to shoot video films on VHS technology. Due to the limitations of this technology, cinematographers had to shoot movies in sequence from start to finish. For example, if the first scene was to be filmed in the central business district of Tamale and the second scene in Kpilo, the cinematographer would shoot the Tamale scene first and then go to Kpilo to shoot the second scene in that order. This filming process made editing tedious since cinematographers were working with limited technology.

Eventually, Alhassan Iddrisu Dawuni (Afa Digital) introduced visual effects with his first scene where a character was made to vanish and appear. Film editing and graphics were done sequentially, where filmmakers and cinematographers edited scenes before they were filmed. For example, to develop the intro and credits of a movie, the filmmaker or cinematographer would write the name of the actor on a blackboard with chalk, film it, and then erase it and write the next thing and then film it, and so on. Others would write the credits on a large piece of cardboard, decorate it with flamboyant flowers, and then shoot it. Therefore, due to limited resources, pioneers were compelled to find innovative ways to do cinematography, editing, design, and visual effects in movie production.

The industry began with the analog era when movies were recorded on VHS and screened at video centers across the Northern Region. This mode of distribution was used with the first Dagbanli movie and subsequent Dagbanli movies until the late 1990s. For a short period in the late 1990s, Ahmed Adam together with Nana Gazor and Kwabena Acheampong of IK Photos facilitated the production of Dagbanli movies on VHS cassettes as movies to take home. Later in the 2000s, the industry began to mass produce and sell movies on DVDs. The industry began to join other industries to sell movies to audiences to take home to view. According to Ahmed Saani (Minister), Iddris Abubakar (Zimboo), and other industry pioneers, the first Dagbanli movie that was made and produced with digital video technology was Iddris Abubakar's *Asadaachi* (2004), with Abdul-Razak Zakaria (Zakvilla) as cinematographer. After *Asadaachi*'s wide success, other filmmakers began to move from analog editing to experimenting with digital technology, and this technology is what has been used in the industry since the 2010s. Today, the industry is shaped by the work that pioneering filmmakers, distributors, and consumers performed to grow and develop it.

Filmmaking, Passion, and Pedagogies

Following the advent of filmmaking in Northern Ghana in 1989, the industry saw tremendous growth. People from various professional backgrounds began picking up the camera to tell the stories of the Dagbamba. The pioneers usually used personal cameras that were made for producing home videos to shoot the early video films. While some pioneering filmmakers joined the industry from related backgrounds where they worked as cinema operators, actors in school plays among others, others drew on their backgrounds in literature to boost their professional work in filmmaking. Ultimately, some pioneers developed an interest in the film industry from being avid fans of Bollywood films that were shown at the cinemas in Tamale. As the industry grew, people who had experience working with other types of media such as radio and photography became interested in the industry.

In the 2020s, some of the major filmmakers in the industry are graduate students, traders, farmers, and teachers, among others. The passion of the early pioneers of the industry and their hard work built and sustained the industry for future filmmakers to add their voices. Even though the second wave of filmmakers and producers follow the thematic and aesthetic conventions in film production in the industry, a few are gradually building their artistic voices as auteur filmmakers. Although there is a tremendous number of stakeholders in the industry today, it is important to note that many of these filmmakers are self-taught and have very little education in the art of filmmaking (Meyer, 2015). This mode of self-teaching coupled with limited access to film production technology resulted in filmmakers employing innovative strategies in growing film technology and film production in the region.

As discussed earlier, the stakeholders of the industry went to extraordinary lengths to produce, edit, and distribute films to audiences. These extraordinary innovative strategies are reflected in the evolution of film technology, picture quality, marketing and advertising, and distribution strategies. I elaborate on these innovative strategies later in the book. Although there is room to further develop these strategies and skills, it is imperative to acknowledge the hard work the pioneers put into the birth and growth of the industry. While others may be fixated on the "poor (video) quality" of films produced by movie industries like Kumawood and the Dagbanli film industry, in this book I am concerned with unpacking how these industries reflect the lived reality of the communities they represent and the symbolism they hold in the cultural mythos of these communities.

Here, I present the various ways in which self-taught filmmakers developed their art and craft as stakeholders in the industry. As we saw earlier, my conversations with many filmmakers indicated that they had no prior training in filmmaking and ultimately taught themselves. Many attributed their knowledge to the foundation built by pioneering filmmakers that paved the way for them to participate in telling the stories of the community through film. For others, their passion for film led them to do everything they could to learn about the art of filmmaking. This is what pioneering female filmmaker Sherifatu Issah had to say about her career journey and the philosophy that has often guided her work:

If you are passionate about something, even if you don't have a teacher, you learn it on your own. Nobody sat me down to teach me anything about films. I am observant. I observe people and can tell what role will best suit them if I cast them in my movies. So, I have my own group of men and women [drama group] that I teach and mentor. All the people who learned from me stand out when they go on location. When you take them to location and ask them to act a certain way, they will do an excellent job of it. It's my passion that has enabled me to support younger people to grow in the industry.

While some filmmakers learned on the job and from pioneering filmmakers, a few upcoming filmmakers like Leonard Kubaloe (aka OBL) learned via social media: "I have taught myself and almost every day I learn. I go on YouTube. It's actually my personal teacher. But of late, I have come to realize that some few tutorials on YouTube teach you the wrong thing. Yes, but a lot of good stuff is on YouTube. I am actually a self-taught filmmaker. I have never had any professional training at all, and I am still learning." This self-taught filmmaker asserted that while social media platforms like YouTube could be useful for learning, it was imperative for learners to be able to discern correct knowledge from wrong knowledge as the information put on some of these sites may be inaccurate.

One of the early filmmakers whose work has been extensively influenced by Bollywood asserts that his interest in filmmaking was sparked by consuming Indian romance musicals. Consuming and enjoying Bollywood films motivated Iddris Abubakar (aka Zimboo) to join the Dagbanli movie industry:

I used to love films a lot and I enjoyed Indian films. They were my favorite. That's what made me drop out of school. We used to sneak into Rivoli Cinema to watch because we couldn't afford the tickets. When they opened a video center in Mr. Razak's house in Polɔya Fɔŋ we snuck in there too to watch the films. One day they were showing a Shaakaa film after the showing of a Dagbanli film and Mr. Razak said that we could also try to make the Dagbanli films. I asked how we could get into the industry. He said he had a store and he would talk to Mr. Halid who would help us. So he shared the idea and we started work on our own films in the industry.

Ultimately, many filmmakers had some interests (however remote) in the media industry and these interests were actualized by becoming part of the Dagbanli video film industry. Others discovered their passion and talent for acting from the dramas they staged during Maulidi (the graduation ceremony at Islamic religious schools in the region). During Maulidis, students participated in various activities such as poetry recitals, singing, drama, choreographed dances, and others. For many students, their first exposure to staged arts and culture was at the Maulidis that were held at their schools. Hamidu Fuseini's (aka Nba Gomda) career in arts and culture started at the Maulidi:

In the house here, we had Maulidis all the time. Yearly, when we were to perform at the Maulidi, we do some acts. So through that people liked my roles. Every year, we do some short drama. By then we were just calling it acting that's in the '70s. From 1970 to 1975 that was my elementary school days. After my form 4 [education], I couldn't go further. So I went and then tried to learn how to sew. By then every night I was in Arabic school for Maulidi rehearsals. So, during the revolution days, an NGO came to educate people on guinea worm disease. When they selected them, I was not in town. They asked of me and I wasn't in town so they . . . that was our first educational film in the north here even though there were so many films.

Others who had done some work in staged plays and dramas eventually joined the industry as actors and filmmakers. Beyond Maulidis, many young filmmakers learned from older pioneering filmmakers who contributed to the growth of the industry. Pioneering filmmakers usually transmitted knowledge about filmmaking to the younger generation. They used this opportunity to learn various skills from others. According to Abdul-Razak Zakaria, he learned film shooting from his father, Zakvilla, who was one of the pioneering filmmakers in the region. He learned how to use a computer in film production from Parinjani, and Alhassan Iddrisu Dawuni taught him visual effects. Much like the pioneering filmmakers in this industry, some Ghallywood filmmakers also found their way into the industry through their work at video centers and cinemas, acting in small theater productions among other activities (Meyer, 2015).

In the early 2020s, there were opportunities for industry stakeholders to formally learn about filmmaking through workshops organized by various organizations in the Ghana film industry. Beyond learning from pioneers and self-teaching, the president of NORDRAFIM (at the time of data gathering in 2018), Alhassan Yushawu Jahanfo, shared that a series of workshops had been organized by industry stakeholders in the past ten years to provide education on the use of basic film technology and basic techniques in acting. In June 2018, another workshop was organized to teach basic skills and knowledge on acting, directing, and filmmaking for members of NORDRAFIM.

In addition to workshops and learning from the elders, the Dagbanli movie industry has filmmakers from diverse backgrounds who bring their knowledge from related backgrounds to their work in filmmaking. All these strategies have contributed to the growth and evolution of the industry. Although many budding filmmakers cannot afford formal training in filmmaking, members of the older generation serve as mentors and resources to the younger ones to develop their careers. Increasingly, workshops where stakeholders undergo training in

FIGURE 3 Victory Cinema. (Photo by Kwame Acheampong, 2018.)

film have become common and have complemented the nonconventional methods used by filmmakers to support their knowledge in filmmaking. It is important to note therefore that the film industry grew tremendously under the unconventional skills of filmmakers who found innovative ways to use available technology to tell stories.

Cultural Flows from Mumbai to Tamale

While media studies scholarship has examined cultural flows from the Global North to the Global South, it is imperative to examine the ways in which media and culture have historically flowed and are presently flowing within the Global South (Adamu, 2010; Larkin, 2008). Bollywood occupies an important position in the Dagbanli movie industry because many film consumers have been exposed to foreign films from North America, South Asia, and South East Asia. According to pioneers in this industry, Bollywood cinema was particularly popular with audiences in the Northern Region. (See figure 3.)

Indeed, some of the key pioneers and stakeholders in the Dagbanli movie industry confessed in interviews that they were avid fans of Indian films before and even after the establishment of the Dagbanli movie industry. Ahmed Adam (aka Mr. Razak) was widely popular among his peers for his ability to memorize and sing the songs from the Bollywood musicals he watched. Others like Ahmed Saani (aka Minister) worked as a video operator in the 1980s at the

Victory Cinema and developed an interest in Bollywood through his professional work.

Although Kannywood, Northern Nigeria's Hausa video film industry based in Kano, was also influenced by Bollywood (Adamu, 2007), according to the filmmakers I spoke with, there was no interaction between the Hausa industry and the Dagbanli industry. Some Dagbanli filmmakers, however, revealed that they studied English-language Nollywood video films to improve their craft. Ultimately, Bollywood cinema influences shaped the musical genre in the industry, and this genre was widely developed by filmmakers like Ahmed Adam, Ahmed Saani, and Iddris Abubakar. Today, Bollywood-influenced Dagbanli movies are associated with these industry pioneers. One of my interlocutors, Alhassan Iddrisu Dawuni, believed that marriages were destroyed by Indian films because young married women spent more time in the cinemas than they did performing their "wifely" duties. Per my conversations with industry stakeholders (filmmakers, distributors, and viewers), film viewing in this community was perceived as an immoral activity. This perception therefore fed the notion that married women who indulged in cinematic film viewing were participating in acts of immorality. This framing of the cinema and film as a site for immorality was not unique to Muslim-majority communities in Northern Ghana; Larkin (2008, p. 91) found that in Northern Nigeria "commercial cinemas were seen as socially disreputable, the place where profligates, idlers and bad Muslims went."

Despite these negative perceptions about Indian movies, they eventually became a big part of the cultural memory and present of the inhabitants of the Northern Region. This means that Bollywood's influence in Northern Ghana extends beyond film and music into cultural facets such as marriage ceremonies, a phenomenon I discuss later in the chapter. Other filmmakers asserted that the popularity of Bollywood films in the Northern Region was because the themes explored in these films shared proximity with the cultures in the Northern Region. Filmmakers quickly learned that infusing Bollywood styles in Dagbanli movies would appeal to audiences who had already taken a liking to Bollywood cinema: "Surprisingly, the cultures and traditions of the Indians depicted in the films are similar to the cultures and traditions of Dagbamba. So, if you are smart you can use the Indian film plot to make a Dagbanli film without people noticing. You don't just copy everything word for word, but you take the plot and use your own culture and tradition to replicate it in Dagbanli. Our films are similar to theirs, but we make them specific and relevant to our culture and tradition" (Sherifatu Issah). Sherifatu Issah's description of the creative process of Dagbanli filmmakers who were inspired by Bollywood can be understood within the context of discussions around glocalization. Here, the film formats are adopted, adapted, and localized to suit the context of the Northern Region. This observation draws attention to South-South media flows, which have not been extensively studied in the context of West Africa. In chapter 5, I expound on these relationships while analyzing the power politics embedded in these connections. Another filmmaker confirmed that drawing on the Bollywood cinematic style to produce Dagbanli video films was a big hit because of the cultural proximity.

Conversations with Sherifatu Issah and Iddris Abubakar indicate that filmmakers were inspired by the Bollywood film style and neither set out nor intended to plagiarize these Indian films. The filmmakers were cognizant of the complexities of artistic inspiration and made sure to point that out during interviews. These cultural flows shaped by cultural proximity to and affinity for Bollywood cinemas meant that some Dagbanli filmmakers glocalized Bollywood films to suit the sociocultural context within which they were operating. Their movies replicated the themes in Bollywood romance musicals. For example, in *Asadaachi* (Iddris Abubakar Zimboo, 2004), a Dagbanli romance musical, the theme of youthful love is extensively explored. The movie is speckled with various musical performances from the two characters Shaakira and Mr. Razak (who profess their love for each other in song lyrics). The musical sections have a distinct Bollywood style and sound, although the lyrics are in Dagbanli. That this Bollywood-inspired genre was popular with audiences meant that a distinct genre that drew on Bollywood sounds was developed in the early industry of the region. This development is similar to the ways in which Bollywood shaped the growth of music genres in Northern Nigeria (Adamu, 2010). Many actors who gained fame from these movies forged lucrative musical careers in this genre per the demands of audiences. Therefore, for many filmmakers Bollywood was the standard against which they measured the quality of their work: "We learned our style of acting and singing from the Indian movies. Therefore, most of our songs use the Indian rhythm. You can use the Indian rhythm without copying the song's instrumentals. I can create my own Indian rhythm for a song from scratch. And I can sue people who copy the instrumentals to make their music because it is my intellectual property, I created it" (Ahmed Adam aka Mr. Razak). While a few pioneering filmmakers were motivated and inspired by Bollywood, it is imperative to note that the first Dagbanli movie was *not* inspired by Bollywood. The first video film, *ɲuni Taali* (Abubakari Sadiq, 1989), explored the politics of relationships in a marital household, contextualizing it within the city of Tamale. Many Dagbanli movies produced today follow the format of the epic that is widely popular in Nollywood and Ghallywood. These epics examine topics that touch on village life (Meyer, 2015) and are often interspersed with comedic scenes to entertain viewers. In fact, Bollywood-inspired movies although popular were and still are just a fraction of the types of movies produced in this industry. In the past decade, we have seen fewer and fewer Bollywood-inspired movies being made since filmmakers are focusing on amplifying the richness of their Indigenous cultures. As one filmmaker noted, the Dagbanli movie industry was inspired by Dagbaŋ cultures and traditions, Bollywood, and other film traditions in Africa and beyond: "We don't condemn other film industries because as an actor you have to keep an open mind when it comes to learning from other industries with regards to acting, style etc. Bollywood is where we learned a lot about film. But not everyone in this industry follows this trajectory. Indian movie fans here also motivate us to learn from this industry" (Ahmed Saani aka Minister). In the 2020s, although Bollywood influences can be noted in some of the Dagbanli movies produced in the Northern Region, movies set in villages that depict the cultures and traditions of the Dagbamba dominate the market. The industry, in this way, follows the trajectory of the evolution of epic films in Nollywood which was later adopted by Ghallywood (Meyer, 2015) and has had tremendous influence in other African film industries. These epic films documented village life and often attempted to depict the traditions and cultures of the communities in which they were set. These movies often inspired a sense of nostalgia in viewers for the "simple village life."

In the 2010s, Bollywood culture flowed into the Ghanaian mediascape through television shows like *Kumkum Bhagya* (Ekta Kapoor, 2014), often broadcast on (satellite) television stations and terrestrial TV stations with nationwide coverage. From my observations of TV viewing culture across Ghana in the 2010s, these shows had grown dedicated audience bases beyond Ghana's Northern Region and their cultural flows manifested in other African national contexts. Around this time, it was not uncommon to find Indian TV shows dubbed in Akan for TV audiences in Southern Ghana. The dubbing of foreign media in Indigenous languages means that they are more accessible to audiences who do not speak English. This phenomenon means that Bollywood is accessed by a unique group of viewers who are usually left out in foreign content consumption in Ghana since media in languages other than English are usually dubbed in English or presented with English subtitles.

Marginalization and Media Development

Despite drawing on Indigenous knowledge systems and culture, to enrich Dagbanli movies there are many challenges that threaten the continued growth of the industry. One of the major challenges identified by filmmakers in the industry was lack of funding to support film projects. All the filmmakers I interviewed asserted that they struggled to secure funding for their projects. Out of the eleven filmmakers with whom I had conversations, only one shared that he secured a bank loan to support his work; the rest funded their projects from their own pockets or borrowed money from producers, friends, or family. Artists in Ghana have always struggled to access resources to support their work. The Ghana government has shown little interest in supporting the arts, so artists are constantly compelled to find innovative ways to fund their projects. Audience enthusiasm for media in their own language means that Indigenous-language movies and other media when supported by the government can draw audiences to state-funded public media, which is fast losing audiences due to a range of factors including poor entertainment programming.

Most filmmakers also work as farmers, teachers, traders, civil service workers, radio presenters, and so on to supplement their filmmaking careers. Other filmmakers lamented the limited support from government, investors, and non-profit organizations in supporting the industry. This finding is in line with research that shows that Ghallywood filmmakers have little to no governmental support to sustain the industry (Aveh, 2010; Meyer, 2015). According to them, the government has never financially supported filmmaking in the industry: "I think we don't have any investors. But the unfortunate thing is also that you cannot have access to any bank loans, which I think the government should have been doing. Because if you look at our number, you will realize that we are also contributing our quota as far as getting the youth employed is concerned but nobody seems to be helpful in that direction" (Alhassan Yushawu Jahanfo). It was rare for filmmakers to even secure loans from banks to support their work. Most filmmakers funded their movies by saving money from their day jobs: "I have not seen one producer who is taking money from the banks or loan. I am saying I have not seen, maybe they are doing it, but I have not seen. Most of them are traders and most of them are government workers so they depend on their salaries. They contribute [money] and then produce, and others too are farmers based on their harvest, they use their money and most of them are butchers and most of them too they depend on other traders" (Alhaji Rashid Bawa aka BBC). Here, BBC laments the limited access to funding via the banking industry, which has strict requirements for securing loans. These strict requirements mean that many filmmakers and producers are unable to secure loans. This filmmaker recounts his struggles to secure funding for his movie and how that impacted the timeline to release: "When I finished *Asadaachi* (2004) and had no money left to release it I put it on hold and went to do some groundnut farming to raise money. I was a video operator at the time, and I rented a generator on credit to run the video business . . . so when I gathered money to pay for the generator, the money got lost on my way back. So, I had to go back to the farm. That's why it took so long to finish this movie" (Iddris Abubakar aka Zimboo). Despite these challenges, stakeholders in the industry have persevered and found ways to sustain the industry. Other filmmakers found other ways of securing funding by approaching people in their social networks to support their projects. Often, these artists were unable to secure funding from these external sources. Some filmmakers observed that producers like Hajia Jumain have been open to providing funding for their projects. This producer provides funding on specific terms that filmmakers and directors are expected to meet so that she can recoup her capital and make some profit: "Others . . . like Haji Jumain some people bring her their stories/scripts and she sponsors them. When she sponsors the film, the balance left then she will keep it. Sometimes she can buy the rights to a film, give the filmmaker some of the money to make the film. Once the film is done then she pays the rest of the money" (Ahmed Saani aka Minister). Other filmmakers like Sherifatu Issah argued that the government should have been a major stakeholder in funding the industry since they believe the industry has contributed to reducing the migration of young people from rural Northern Ghana to urban Southern Ghana for *kayayo* (where young women carry luggage for a small fee). "Even kayayo, people come back from kayayo but because we [industry stakeholders] work with them they don't go back to the South to do that type of work. They stay back as actors. Some who have intentions of going come and work with us and change their minds about migrating to the South for greener pastures. We help the young women and men to turn away from social vices so the government should pay attention to our work and help us because we have done a lot of work to reduce social vices." Sherifatu Issah believes that the industry has the potential to serve as a catalyst for social change by recruiting marginalized young people, especially women, to prevent migration to the South where they face physical, psychological, and sexual abuse while working as kayayo. However, it is unclear what the statistics say about the industry's contribution to the reduction of the migration of Northern youth to the South for menial jobs under dehumanizing conditions.

Despite the financial challenges faced by filmmakers, they have been able to work to keep the industry alive by securing funds through savings from their day jobs. It is unclear how long the industry will be able to sustain these sources of funding over time. Limited access to financial resources has been blamed by filmmakers for the poor quality of the movies produced. Many filmmakers believe that if the industry continues to release subpar movies, it will eventually lose most of its audience base. Some interlocutors asserted that the industry has lost audiences due to low-quality productions over the years and that stakeholders will have to work on various intervention strategies to regain these audiences since audiences are increasingly exposed to better quality media products from elsewhere. Both distributors and audiences have attributed the gradual demise of the industry to low video and plot quality, among other factors.

Cinemas, Culture, and Globalization

While there have been extensive discussions on cultural flows across the world, there is the need to examine cultural flows within the Global South and how these flows have shaped popular culture today (Adamu, 2010; Virdi, 2017).

Drawing on African Indigenous knowledge systems (Mohammed, 2022a) to understand the historical and present context of film in Global South countries like Ghana is imperative to understand the nuances in the thematic and aesthetic aspects of film. This perspective also sheds light on the cultural flows within the Global South that were/are not a reactionary response to Western cinemas but an organic nurturing of a relationship fed by cultural and religious proximity among other things. These flows demonstrate the agency of film audiences and how this agency intertwines with their media consumption habits. While some may argue that this phenomenon is a product solely of globalization, I argue that film audiences here are not mindless consumers; rather, they complicate the notion of globalization when their film reception habits are culturally and socially situated.

It is important to note that the growth of the industry was directly connected to the growth of drama groups, some of which traveled from village to village to stage educational and entertaining plays. The existence of drama groups in the industry today can be traced to the formation of the Biehisuŋ Drama Group, which set the tone for the growth of drama group culture in the Dagbanli movie industry. Similarly, the growth of the Nigerian video film industry has been attributed to Yoruba traveling cinema and the extensive work that Yoruba theater artists did to support the birth and evolution of video film in Nigeria (Olayiwola, 2011).

In conversations about global media flows, it is important to note that cultural products in the form of Bollywood films, American westerns and Chinese kung fu films were enjoyed by African audiences. While Adamu (2007, p. 83) found that some Bollywood-influenced films in the Hausa movie industry in Northern Nigeria followed a process to "rip-off Indian Masala films and remake them into Hausa copies," the data in this study show that filmmakers were inspired by Bollywood and did not directly lift Bollywood storylines to create art. It is however imperative to note that there is the possibility that some filmmakers in this industry may have ripped off Bollywood storylines to make Dagbanli films.

In this chapter, I have demonstrated that beyond Bollywood cultural flows to Muslim-majority countries in Africa like Nigeria, Morocco, and Senegal, Bollywood films were popular in Muslim communities Ghana. According to Adamu (2010) and Larkin (2008), Indian films were popular in Muslim Northern Nigeria because of the cultural proximity between the themes depicted in the films and the lives of Hausa Northern Nigerians. While there are differences in the ways that Bollywood shaped film in Northern Ghana and Northern Nigeria, existing scholarship (Adamu, 2007) and evidence from conversations with interlocutors demonstrate that Bollywood inspired the thematic and aesthetic aspects of the romance musical film genre in both the Dagbanli and Hausa movie industries. Filmmakers in the Dagbanli movie industry identified cultural proximity as the major reason for the popularity of Bollywood movies in Northern Ghana. Ultimately, cultural flows from Bollywood to Northern Nigeria and Northern Ghana seemed to be happening simultaneously. Filmmakers in Northern Ghana however clarified that there was no direct contact between Kannywood and the Dagbanli movie industry. These Bollywood cultural flows ultimately contributed to the development of musical genres shaped by Bollywood music in Northern Nigeria (Adamu, 2010). Similarly, the incorporation of Bollywood music styles in romance musical movies in Northern Ghana spilled into the music industry for a period of time and significantly shaped an aspect of the Dagbanli romantic music genre. This genre has declined in popularity in the past decade.

Although Bollywood films have waned in popularity on the continent for various reasons, Indian TV shows such as *Kumkum Bhagya* (Ekta Kapoor, 2014) have increasingly become popular with Ghanaian audiences (*India TV News*, 2017) since the 2000s. In 2017, several cast members of *Kumkum Bhagya* visited Ghana to meet and interact with their fans in Accra, Kumasi, and Tamale (*Ghanaweb*, 2017). The popularity of these shows means that they are often dubbed in Ghanaian languages like Akan on TV stations located in the South of Ghana and discussion forums are held on these TV stations after each episode to discuss matters arising from the show. Bollywood influences on culture are still evident today in the cultural and material memory of Tamale in the form of events like weddings. Since the 2000s, Northern Ghanaian Muslim couples have worn Bollywood-inspired Indian clothing known as "Indian wear" to their marriage ceremonies. Here, the cultural flows are not just limited to movies but spill into other cultural facets such as weddings and fashion.

Media Production, Epistemologies, and the Future

This chapter has parsed out the history of Dagbanli movies in Northern Ghana and the ways in which the industry participates in cultural flows in the Global South. Drawing on Indigenous knowledge systems to guide the deconstruction of conversations with interlocutors means that the perspectives of locals and the collective memory of key stakeholders are centered in this narrative. This framework also creates room for a more nuanced understanding of the evolution of film in colonial and postcolonial Ghana and the ways in which ethnic and cultural resistance have manifested in sustaining the movie industry. There continues to be a dearth of research on Indigenous-language media in Africa, and more work needs to be done to fill this epistemological gap.

In this chapter, I have opened ways to theorize Indigenous-language media shedding light on the intricacies of individual, industry, and collective memory. This chapter has built on chapter 1's strategies to navigate epistemology in Indigenous communities in Ghana. These strategies may be extrapolated to apply to culturally similar contexts in the Global South. In transcribing data from Indigenous languages to English, it is imperative to draw on interdisciplinary perspectives to address the complexities of these epistemologies. Here, I demonstrate the importance of representing and centering historically marginalized perspectives and diverse voices in scholarship. Translation theory can provide the necessary tools to translate data from Indigenous languages to English and vice versa while preserving the aura of the language and unique personality traits of interlocutors (Mohammed, 2019).

To address the challenges faced by the Dagbanli movie industry and ensure its growth, the government of Ghana should invest in supporting the arts. Publicly funded media are often mandated to produce media for the public good. These standards can be applied to movies funded using resources provided by taxpayers. Although governmental influence may curtail the creative freedoms of filmmakers and producers whose movies are funded by the public, independent regulatory bodies like the National Media Commission can be tasked with instituting checks and balances to support the creative freedoms of artists. Nonprofits and multinational organizations should also offer support to the arts industry to ensure the sustenance of Indigenous-language arts. Support may take the form of funding film projects and supporting already existing training programs to help filmmakers, producers, and distributors improve their work. The industry may collaborate with media and communication programs in educational institutions like the University for Development Studies and the Tamale Technical University in the form of working with already existing internship programs for students; industry stakeholders could also lecture and speak at colloquia to bridge the gap between theory and praxis.

In this chapter, I examined the history of the Dagbanli movie industry by contextualizing it within the global media economy. Here, I draw on and complement the oral histories and collective memories about the movie industry. The findings show that the Dagbanli movie industry was established for similar reasons for which the English-language movie industries in Ghana (Aveh, 2010) and Nigeria (Onuzulike, 2007) were established: to mediate the lived reality of local audiences. Here, I contribute to scholarship on cultural flows within the Global South that have not been extensively studied. Discussions from this chapter support previous work (Adamu, 2007; Barlet, 2010) on Bollywood cultural flows to Muslim communities in Africa.

5

Movie Distribution, Urban Architecture, and the Newsification of Movies

• •

Kookali lana n wumdi jɛbɔbgi kumsi

Although the growth of film in Africa has been tied to colonization and the desire of the colonizer to use it to control Indigenous people, film has grown and evolved tremendously especially in West Africa. This growth means that anglophone cinemas in Ghana and Nigeria are increasingly gaining visibility not only at home but on the global stage, with Ghanaian films being submitted to and nominated for American awards such as the Academy Awards and the Golden Globes in 2019. While we attempt to understand the growing popularity of African movies globally, it is imperative to critically study the ways in which these films are consumed on and off the continent. Increasingly Nollywood is finding its way to streaming platforms such as Netflix, while growing cinema culture by way of film premieres at home. The same can be said of the Ghanaian film industry, which is struggling to catch up with its Nigerian counterpart on the global stage. In recent times, Ghallywood films such as *Azali* (Kwabena Ghansah, 2018) and *The Burial of Kojo* (Sam "Blitz" Bazawule, 2018), which extensively incorporate Indigenous languages like Dagbanli and Twi, respectively, have found their way to streaming platforms such as Netflix.

While we pay attention to the growth of African cinemas in the age of new media and streaming platforms, it is imperative to examine which types of film industries are representing the continent globally. While anglophone cinemas in Ghana and Nigeria are extensively theorized and discussed in popular culture, Indigenous-language cinemas, which are constantly marginalized nationally but have historically been accessible to audiences, are increasingly erased from the conversation (Mohammed, 2025). For example, research on film in Ghana disproportionately focuses on the predominantly English-language Ghallywood while ignoring the potential and extensive audience reach of Indigenous-language film industries.

Beyond film, Indigenous-language media in general has been largely marginalized on the continent, as we saw in chapter 4, and this can be tied to the colonial framing of African languages, cultures, and traditions as savage and in need of taming and saving by the white (neo)colonizer. Through a decolonial approach, I position Indigenous-language film industries within national contexts, connecting them to the violence of colonization that sought to strip Africans of their historical, cultural, and linguistic identities. Here, Indigenous film industries are deconstructed as sites of resistance to colonization, focusing on their ability to demarginalize African languages that are gradually suffering linguicide especially within the diaspora and among the urban African middle class.

In this chapter, we pay critical attention to the channels of distribution in the Dagbanli movie industry, making connections and juxtapositions between this industry and other national, regional, and global film industries. I argue here that to understand the struggles Indigenous-language filmmakers face in marketing and distributing their movies, it is imperative to map the historical trajectory of these industries to current contextual factors of marginalization and colonization and how they shape film distribution locally and transnationally.

Cinema Cultures in Nigeria and Ghana

Films in colonial anglophone Africa were positioned didactically to shape the thinking of locals. That films were utilized for colonial propaganda meant that the Colonial Film Unit mostly produced documentary and educational films for locals. According to Smyth (2013), films produced by the Colonial Film Unit in "West Africa between 1945 and 1951 demonstrate attempts at the social reconstruction of the rural African in political, social, and economic ways modelled on Western culture" (p. 94). Smyth (2013) indicates that the establishment of the Accra Film School in 1949 meant that there was a steady growth in the production of educational and feature films such as *Amenu's Child* (1950), *The Boy Kumasenu* (1952), *Progress in Kojokrom* (1953), and *Mr. Mensah Builds a House* (1955). Interestingly, all the films listed here attempted to capture the attention of colonized subjects using names of cities and people in Southern Ghanaian cultures. This centering of Southern Ghanaian cultures in national media representations persists today. In this book, therefore, I draw attention to subaltern media by re-righting the silenced histories of media in Ghana focusing specifically on Northern Ghana.

Post-independence, film viewing culture in cinemas became vibrant where audiences were treated to American action films, Chinese films and Bollywood films. Among other reasons, these political disruptions (coups d'état) coupled with curfews that restricted the movement of people after dusk disrupted cinema viewing culture and ultimately stagnated the cinema industry, which was suspended during these types of political unrest. Before long, cinema halls had been sold to churches, ultimately mitigating cinema-going culture in the country (Meyer, 2015).

By 1985, the Ghanaian film industry had grown steadily, garnering many audiences with the representations of themes that were relatable to the people. According to Aveh (2014), it is imperative to examine the Nigerianization of Ghanaian eyes in our attempts to deconstruct the complexities of Ghanaian audiences and understand the decline of the movie industry. Eventually, movies were sold to take home, shifting film viewing from cinemas to film viewing at home (Meyer, 2015). Cinema going has started to pick up since the early 2000s with the establishment of Silverbird Cinemas in the Accra Mall, among other factors. Filmmakers across the country are beginning to create temporary cinemas out of alternative spaces such as seminar halls, hotel auditoriums, and open-air spaces to screen their movies commercially.

Despite attempts to break away from the violent colonial history of film in postcolonies, the film landscape is currently organized hierarchically privileging movie industries that have the most proximity to the colonizer via language and culture. Therefore, the very existence of Indigenous-language film industries is an act of resistance and a constant reminder of the denigration and demonization of African languages and cultures. Throughout this chapter, I draw on decolonial approaches to critically examine the role that Indigenous-language film industries play via distribution in demarginalizing African languages, cultures, and realities.

Continental and National Networks of Distribution

For various reasons, many filmmakers and industry stakeholders have constantly struggled with marketing and finding sustainable ways of distributing their art beyond their local communities. These challenges in distribution coupled with other contextual factors that constrained cinema-going culture led to the development of film distribution networks via VHS tapes, video CDs, and DVDs. This challenge is identical to film industries across West Africa and is particularly evident in the film scenes in Ghana and Nigeria. While a few filmmakers have access to and are able to screen their movies in cinemas in

Accra, the majority of filmmakers in the subaltern industries do not have access to these opportunities, pointing to a hierarchy in the industry that privileges Ghallywood and auteur filmmakers and producers over filmmakers and producers in Indigenous-language cinema spaces.

According to scholars, the few corporations that have attempted to address the distribution challenges facing many African film industries have ultimately monopolized the distribution market and disenfranchised African artists in the industry (Mboti and Tomaselli, 2015). Challenges in film distribution pose questions about African film archiving. According to Fisher (2018), an attempt at preserving and archiving African films on digital platforms by the Electronic Media Network (M-Net) through the African Film Library was a short-lived project that lasted only a year. M-Net's project was a video-on-demand (VOD) library aimed at preserving and archiving classic African films (Fisher, 2018). M-Net's business model was exploitative of African filmmakers and was perhaps one of many reasons why this digital archival project failed (Fisher, 2018). It is also imperative to note that this archival project was exclusionary in that filmmakers in subaltern industries across the continent rarely had access to these platforms to market and stream their work.

Beyond the exploitation of African filmmakers and stakeholders by multinational corporations, many filmmakers still grapple with addressing the issues of piracy that are common across the continent. The rapid growth of digital media use has caused wide speculation about the importance of digital media to film distribution. In making these speculations, it is imperative to consider that there is still a wide digital divide on the continent, and for most Indigenous-language film audiences specifically, this divide excludes them from digital consumption of media. In addition, despite the seeming rise in the "now-familiar services of iTunes, Netflix and Amazon Instant" (Fisher, 2018, p. 240), only a few African video films and TV series (mostly from Nigeria and South Africa) make it to streaming platforms like Netflix. In fact, since 2016 Netflix has worked on developing and acquiring content from South Africa and later (2020) in Nigeria. And their work in these markets is publicized by the Twitter accounts dedicated to the streamer's work in these countries. Interestingly much of the African film market is left out of these expansion efforts, with very little attention paid to expanding and developing content to cater to the needs of francophone audiences and African audiences who speak only Indigenous languages. Here, Anglo-American dominance has a tremendous influence on market and production decisions made by the global streamer in targeting their African audiences.

To make it to Netflix, filmmakers should have access to the most advanced filmmaking technology to even be considered; cultural capital plays a critical role in determining who has access to Netflix and who doesn't, again pointing to a hierarchy on the continent. Indeed, digital streaming of films is still not accessible to many Africans due to the high costs of internet data, limited access to streaming technologies, and a lack of technological and digital literacy. Beyond digital media access, digital platforms have not exactly revolutionized film distribution in Africa but have given way to the monopolization of distribution by a handful of gatekeepers, again compounding the already existing hierarchies in these industries.

Indigenous Knowledge, Film Distribution, and Marketing

Since its inception in 1989, the Dagbanli movie industry has found innovative ways to sustain the industry in production, distribution, and reception while attempting to stay true to the culture of the region and serving the needs of the community. As seen in earlier chapters, Bollywood and Nollywood have had influences on the aesthetic and thematic aspects of the industry. The marketing of Dagbanli movies has evolved with the growth of the industry in the past few decades. When video films were distributed via screenings at video centers in the early 1990s, audiences would share their impressions of movies with prospective viewers to get them interested in going to watch these movies. This marketing by word of mouth was contingent on the success of the first showing of the movie at a well-known video center.

Before the advent of the Dagbanli movie industry, people like Ahmed Saani (Minister), who lived a few blocks away from Victory Cinema and spent a lot of time there, acted as poster boys for the Indian, American, and Chinese films that were screened there. This mode of advertising was quite popular in the analog era of the 1980s. The filmmaker fondly recalls,

> So the poster was like an advert. We took the poster around to advertise it to potential audiences. They would give us a board with "Victory Cinema" written on it. And then they would write, showing tonight. . . . And then they would put the poster with drawings about the film on the board. We would carry the board and one person would carry a bell and ring it to draw attention to us as we went on the rounds. We would go to the market and make rounds, leave the market and go to the suburbs and make rounds there too. (Ahmed Saani aka Minister, personal communication, 2018)

Scholars have found that advertising foreign video films on hand-painted posters was widely popular in Ghana and Nigeria and is an integral part of the evolution of film in both countries (Schmidt, 2005; Wolfe, 2001). In conversations with my interlocutors, I found that this phenomenon was popular not just in Accra and Kumasi but in other urban areas like Tamale. Figure 4 presents an example of a hand-painted movie poster about a Ghanaian movie, *Diabolo 3* (Bob Smith Jnr, 1992). It is unclear whether these hand-painted

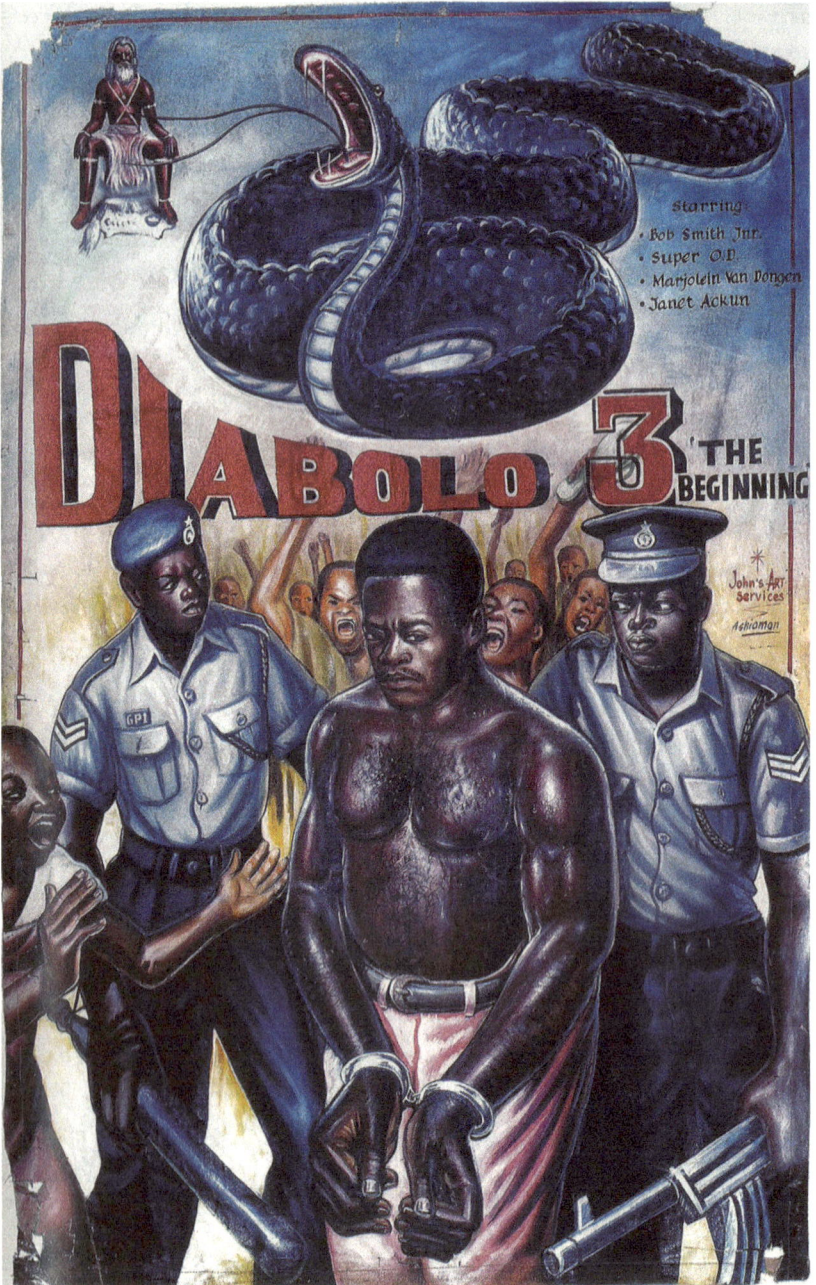

FIGURE 4 Hand-painted movie poster for *Diabolo 3*. (Credit: John's Art Services, Ashiaman.)

posters were used to advertise Dagbanli video films in the late 1980s. When the industry evolved to DVD technology, producers began to advertise through radio announcements and later radio jingles. These radio announcements, which usually ran in Dagbanli and occasionally English, presented a synopsis of the movie and listed the popular actors who were starring in the movie. Radio announcements about new movies were made early in the morning or in the evening (peak listening hours). Radio jingles replicated the structural format of the announcements but made use of known radio voices for the jingles, some of whom were actors in the industry. The movie jingle advertisement has grown into a whole genre where voice actors dramatize the movie by stressing the important parts of the plot, using sound effects, and speaking loudly to draw the attention of the listener. Where applicable, audio scenes from the movie are included in the jingle to give viewers a taste of what the film is about. This strategy has also been used to advertise Kumawood films in the Ashanti Region since the 2000s. Radio announcements and jingles are still used to target both rural and urban audiences.

Since the 2010s, the establishment of satellite TV stations like Sagani TV, North TV (NTV), and Zaa TV has resulted in the placement of movie adverts on television. TV jingles in Dagbanli have been developed based on the radio jingle format with the addition of still images and short scenes from the movies. Although there is a growing use of satellite TV to advertise newly released movies via jingles and media interviews with filmmakers and actors, distributors maintain that radio adverts are still imperative to marketing since a chunk of the audiences who live in rural communities have limited access to satellite television: "Since the TV stations started operating, when we want to run commercials for films, we are asked to pay a lot of money. At first, we played our commercials on radio stations but now you are expected to pay Sagani TV and NTV and then pay radio stations. Because in the villages not everyone has satellite or electricity, they listen to the radio. And those in Bolga or in the South and they can watch NTV or Sagani TV to see our adverts" (Mariam Mohammed, Saɣari Gungɔŋ Productions, personal communication, 2018). Stakeholders in the industry are cognizant of the digital divide and take that into consideration as they work on marketing their movies to a wide array of audiences.

Beyond radio and television advertisements, some filmmakers and producers have taken advantage of platforms like WhatsApp and Facebook to share digital movie posters. These avenues for marketing have proved inaccessible to producers, directors, and actors who have little technological literacy and limited technological access. Therefore, this medium is used by filmmakers whose social capital includes technological literacy and access. However, due to the digital divide, the majority of the audiences who buy movies to take home do not have access to these social media platforms. The poster depicted in figure 5 was retrieved from Iddris Abubakar's (Zimboo) Facebook, where he

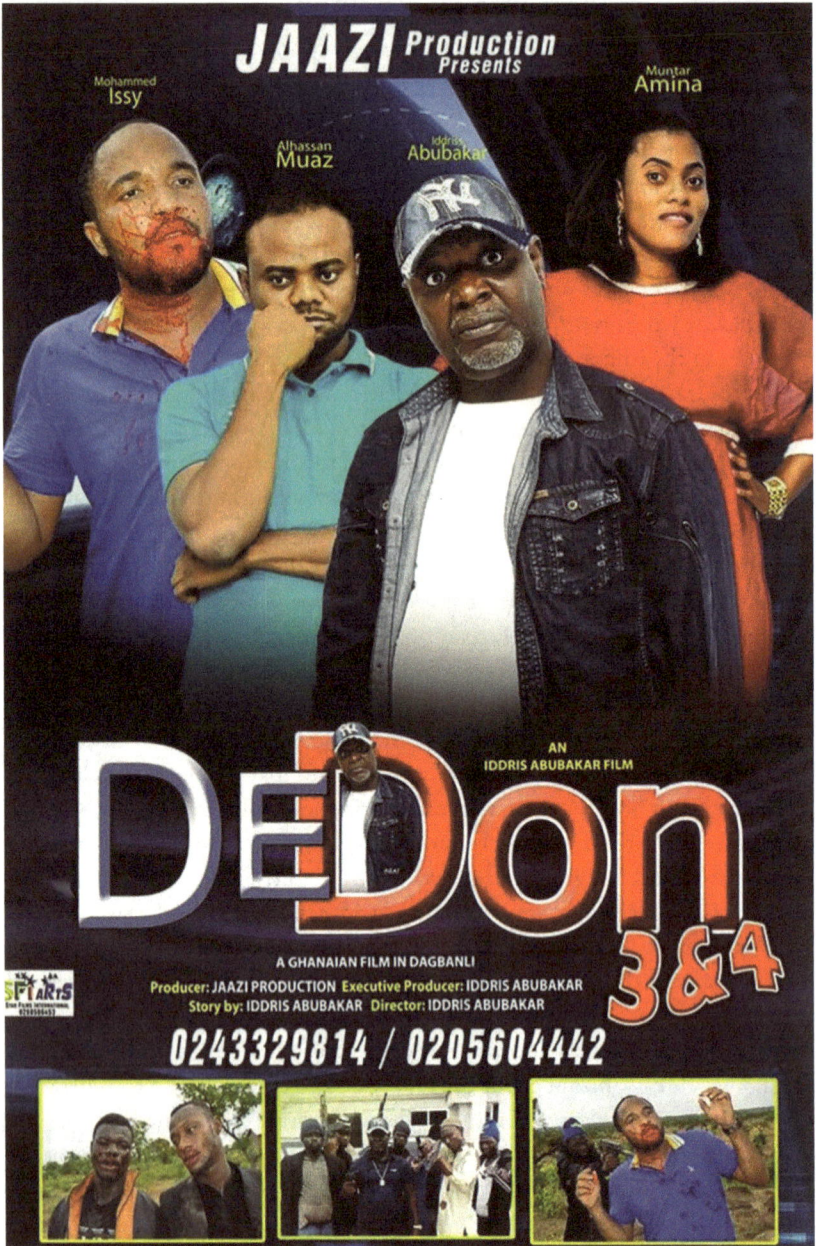

FIGURE 5   Film poster for *De Don*. (Credit: Iddris Abubakar Facebook page, 2018.)

FIGURE 6 Zaa Nsuma store. (Photo by Kwame Acheampong, 2018.)

was marketing his film *De Don* (which means the Don) to his network on social media in 2018.

In addition, banners have become increasingly popular in marketing movies, they are usually projected in the verandah area of distribution stores to advertise upcoming or recently released movies. The banner style of marketing replicates the radio announcement, radio jingle, and TV jingle style where all the pertinent information on the film is presented in a still image to market the film to viewers. Indeed, parallels can be drawn between this marketing strategy and the use of poster boys to market films showing at Victory Cinema in the 1980s. Here, new forms of publicity build on old forms to create new mediums of marketing. These modern posters are glossier and based on photo images, whereas the posters were hand painted by artists. Prior to the release of a film, producers print several banners so that distributors can hang them in front of their stores. The banners pictured in figure 6 were displayed outside Zaa Nsuma's distribution store in the Aboabo Market in Tamale in the rainy season of 2018.

In addition to banners, large paper posters are printed to facilitate sales for vendors who sell in rural communities. When vendors go to distribution shops to buy movies to retail, they are given a couple of paper posters of the film to display to their prospective customers. When I spent time at the Nasara distribution shop, I noticed that a vendor who had come to purchase some DVDs was given paper posters to facilitate his marketing of movies to prospective customers.

Newsification as a Marketing Strategy

While filmmakers may draw inspiration from personal experiences and social observations to support the development of films, there is an increasing trend especially in the Dagbanli- and Twi-language movie industries to draw directly from the news and current events to develop stories for the screen. This is what I call the "newsification of movies." This newsification of stories that have become popular in the public sphere are particularly common in the comedic genre of these industries. In the United States, newsification manifested in the form of television shows drawing heavily on popular current events to shape the plot of their stories. We still see this newsification today when U.S. TV shows cover content on issues popular in the news cycle such as the COVID-19 pandemic, police brutality, and so on. According to Schudson (1991), television "proudly, runs dramatic programs, sit-coms, and soaps that borrow from contemporary controversies for plot material." I posit here that newsification is used in these movie industries as a marketing strategy to appeal to the interest of audiences in current events.

By newsification, I mean that some filmmakers make movies based on sensational news stories. For example, a Dagbanli movie titled *Anas Aremeyaw Anas* was released at the time that investigative journalist Anas Aremeyaw Anas released *Number 12* (in June 2018), an investigative documentary film that revealed the corrupt practices of the Ghana Football Association (GFA). This documentary also brought attention to the corrupt practices of Fédération Internationale de Football Association (FIFA) in Ghana and in other parts of Africa and the world. It is important to note that these newsified movies usually take less than a (few) week(s) to film. To boost sales, filmmakers and producers often work quickly to release them while the issues are still relevant in the news cycle and fresh in the minds of audiences.

Dagbanli movies have been marketed through audiences by word-of-mouth, radio announcements, radio jingles, TV jingles, (digital) posters, banners, and mobile vehicles. These strategies are radically different from the way that auteur and Ghallywood filmmakers currently market their films. Film marketing in this context mirrors the ways that small businesses in this community market and sell their commodities, using radio and TV advertisements, vendors, banners, and posters. That this industry is systematically excluded from so-called formal modes of distribution such as streaming platforms and cinemas means that stakeholders are compelled to find innovative, localized ways of marketing and distributing their movies. This exclusion once again points to a hierarchy in the mediascape in Ghana where Dagbanli filmmakers are excluded due to limited financial access, limited access to technology, limited cultural capital, linguistic and cultural marginalization, and other factors. Ultimately, the very existence and sustenance of the industry is an act of resistance in the face of colonization from national and global actors in the geopolitics of film.

Social Capital and the Politics of Film Distribution

Recent discussions around the growth of streaming services such as Netflix and Amazon Prime Video have focused on the growing interests of these video companies in globalizing their content and expanding their subscriber base beyond the United States. The globalization of Netflix, for example, focused on Latin America, Europe, and Asia between 2010 and 2015 (Lobato, 2019). During this period, Africans were mere spectators of these expansion efforts of the streamer. From 2015 onward, the global streamer broke into the African film market through Nigeria and South Africa. This trend of globalization, where media globalization efforts often reach Africa last demonstrate the continent's positioning in global geopolitics and the Global North's perceptions about the African continent as a "viable" market for entertainment media.

To understand the current state of the movie industry, it is imperative to critically examine the intricacies of film distribution and how distribution strategies situate the Dagbanli movie industry in the hierarchy of film industries nationally and globally. Therefore, Netflix's expansion to the continent privileged English-language film industries like Nollywood. Even within Nollywood, hierarchies of social and cultural capital determined which filmmakers got their work on the streaming platform first. It was not until the late 2010s that we began to see Ghanaian movies on Netflix. Despite this exclusion from global circuits of film distribution, the Dagbanli movie industry has grown to develop a complex network that facilitates the distribution of movies across the country. In recent times, some filmmakers are beginning to embrace uploading their movies to YouTube to facilitate access for the Dagbaŋ diaspora and non-Dagbamba audiences.

Here, I unpack the intricacies of movie distribution in this industry while problematizing issues of access and marginalization. In the past when distributors were put in charge of making copies of movies and releasing them, they would give a stipulated number of DVDs to other major distributors in the network to sell and then pay them after sales. Recently, however, distributors are moving more and more toward a cash-and-carry system where they only release DVDs to other distributors in the network if they are prepared to pay cash up front. Distributors usually pay fellow distributors after they have finished selling their films. In cases where they finish selling the DVDs that are highly patronized, they ask the main distributor of the film for more copies. When they are unable to sell all the DVDs, they gather the copies left and send them back to the main distributor, leaving a few copies for retail.

To keep track of all the movies that are distributed, some distributors maintain records of how many movies they bought from a particular distributor and keep track of the sales made. Distribution shop owners hold regular weekly meetings with vendors to keep account of how their sales are going and check to see if they need to restock on specific movies. If they realize the sales of a particular movie is low, they may take them back from retailers to save them for the producer/distributor when they account for sales. Different distributors have various relationships with vendors. Some vendors are recruited on good faith, while others are asked to pay cash for movie stock upon recruitment. Those who are recruited on good faith can sell DVDs and then pay the shops after selling them. This distributor explained the process of recruiting vendors: "Like today, it may happen that a stranger will enter, and he will tell me he wants to do business and he will be selling the DVDs. But I will say oh that's nice, but I don't know you. So, try to bring someone I know so in case I don't see you I know where to go" (Mohammed Razak, Zaa Nsuma Productions, personal communication, 2018). The process of finding respected individuals to vouch for potential vendors is common within the market ecology of Tamale where interested vendors are introduced to retailers or business owners by community members who serve as guarantors. According to this interlocutor, while some vendors would buy movies upfront, they allowed vendors they trusted to sell DVDs and then pay afterwards. This strategy of using guarantors is a feature of the market landscape of this community. It has been observed among other traders such as clothing and shoe sellers. Vendors are an integral part of the market; they ensure that movies reach viewers in rural areas. Most major distributors have vendors with whom they work exclusively to sell movies beyond Tamale. Movies are distributed by vendors to other parts of the Northern Region like Yendi, Bimbilla, Savelugu, Gushaɣu, and Karaga.

In addition to vendors, the distribution market relied on business models that were based on using the services provided by telecommunications companies like mobile banking services to facilitate the exchange of money among people who have little to no access to traditional banking. Major distributors in Tamale like Nasara, Zample, Zaa Nsuma, and Saɣari Gungɔŋ often have contacts in major towns and cities who they ship DVDs directly to via public transport. In this model, distributors transact business via phone calls and make payments through the increasingly popular mobile money banking system. Movies are often shipped to retailers in other major cities like Accra and Kumasi. (See figure 7).

Despite the complexity of the distribution network in the region, distributors have encountered several hurdles in attempts to market and distribute movies beyond Ghana. Although in recent times some movies have English subtitles to widen the audience reach, pirates are publicly sharing Dagbanli video films on platforms like YouTube without securing the permission of

FIGURE 7 Inside Nasara Productions store. (Photo by Kwame Acheampong, 2018.)

filmmakers. While a few technologically literate filmmakers have been able to have their movies, which have been illegally uploaded to YouTube, taken down for copyright violations, filmmakers who are neither familiar with digital technology nor have access are rarely able to have their pirated movies removed. Ultimately, stakeholders in this industry are not enjoying the dividends of streaming platforms like Netflix widening their reach and operations in the African market. While a few auteur and Ghallywood filmmakers get to sign lucrative deals with Netflix to stream their movies, these local industries are increasingly erased and left out of the conversation, again demonstrating a hierarchy in the industry that streamers like Netflix reproduce.

Gender, Geography, and Viewing Cultures

Despite Netflix's recent forays into the African market with a subscriber base of 2.6 million in 2021, there are still large swaths of African audiences who are not catered to. While Netflix subscriptions in Ghana have risen slowly, several structural factors continue to impede access such as the digital divide. Since the 1940s, audiences across West Africa have watched films via the colonial mobile cinema. In the postcolony, mobile film units moved from town to town and village to village to "show a mix of documentaries, newsreels, and pedagogical dramas intended to instruct audiences about the achievements of the state and educate them in modes of health, farming, and civic participation" (Larkin, 2008, p. 77). After independence, the Information Services

FIGURE 8   Melcom store, formerly Rivoli Cinema. (Photo by Kwame Acheampong, 2018.)

Department was maintained and restructured to use film as an avenue for education and information. This transition meant that the Ghana government led by Dr. Kwame Nkrumah utilized film to promote nationalist propaganda and development.

Although screening culture has been on the rise again since the 2000s, cinema buildings are not being restored. For example, the Victory Cinema building in Tamale was used as a warehouse for goods by the owner at the time of writing. In the 1980s and 1990s, cinemas like Victory formed an important part of the entertainment landscape. Here, Indian, Chinese, and American films were shown on a regular basis. Beyond viewers' engagement with film as informational and educational tools, audiences went out of their way to actively participate in cinema viewing culture by paying to see these foreign films at the two major cinemas in Tamale: Victory and Rivoli. Rivoli Cinema later became home to Pep Stores in the early 2000s and is now home to Melcom Stores, a retail chain with outlets nationwide. (See figure 8.)

Although foreign, especially Indian, films were popular with viewers at the time, there was an explosion in interest in local movies when *ŋuni Taali* (Whose fault?) was released in 1989. The wide interest drawn by early Dagbanli movies stemmed from the excitement that was sparked in viewers when they saw people like them on the screen, speaking the same language as them. This tremendous support from audiences propelled the nascent industry into a vibrant one. Following the release of the first movie in 1989, *Naabaala* (Abdul Rahman Amangai, 1992)—one of the most popular Dagbanli movies of all time—was released and gained wide popularity for years. The desire of audiences to see people like them on screen quickly translated into wide patronage of Dagbanli movies at video centers. Indeed, audience support of the industry has sustained it for decades. According to this distributor, viewers were excited about Dagbanli movies in the early days: "Ooi! They loved the films a lot because they [the films] had lot of energy. That was when the market was booming. When DVD technology was not in use" (Hajia Jumain Ahmed, Zample Productions, personal communication, 2018). Today, viewers buy DVDs to take home for family viewing. While some audiences patronize movies in which their favorite actors appear, others focus on which drama groups are engaged in the production of the film, and for some the topic explored in the film is of utmost importance. "Everyone has their favorites. Some people buy films because of Umar Janda [a popular comedic actor], others buy films because of Zimboo [a popular actor in drama and action movies], there are others who are big fans of Lawyer Gbaɣinli [a popular comedic actor]. Others are fans of Labzorrow or A bori mahim. Everyone has their favorite" (Mariam Mohammed, Saɣari Gungɔŋ Productions, personal communication, 2018). This observation is consistent with the findings in audience communal conversation circles (CCCs) where audiences shared that their favorite actors and filmmakers influenced their movie purchasing habits. For new viewers, distribution shop managers helped them pick out movies that they might enjoy. Beyond factors that viewers consider when purchasing movies, distributors assert that the audience groups that patronize Dagbanli films the most are people living in rural communities and women.

According to all six distributors that I spoke with, people living in rural communities constituted the majority of the audience population that patronized Dagbanli movies. This finding does not necessarily mean that urban dwellers do not watch Dagbanli movies; they watch them via different avenues, which bring no revenue to filmmakers and producers. Distributors assert that viewers in rural communities are the backbone of the movie economy because they are the group that brings in the most sales revenue. This interlocutor explained in detail the role villagers play in boosting sales in the industry: "Naawuni zuɣu, the villagers buy a lot of movies. They come and buy the movies to keep us in business. But in Accra, you can send like a thousand DVDs and for a whole month, they won't pay you and then return your movies back to you. Sometimes they won't return them at all. They will tell you they were only able to sell this amount and then they will pay you for it, but they hold on to the DVDs" (Mariam Mohammed, Saɣari Gungɔŋ Productions, personal communication, 2018). In urban areas, however, viewers resort to illegal sharing of pirated DVDs for viewing. Viewers in urban areas are usually tech savvy and have knowledge of how to access films illegally. Young viewers, especially in cities like Accra and Tamale, share movie files in their network. "Because they are educated, and they know more about computer that's why we have started locking it. It's now better if it's locked so that it can't be copied" (Jumain Ahmed, Zample Productions, personal communication, 2018). This illegal sharing of media extends beyond Dagbanli movies to foreign (Hollywood, Asian, Latin American) films and telenovelas. This illegal sharing means that urban viewers do not have to pay to watch movies on their personal computers. Others also watch the movies by streaming Dagbanli movies that are illegally uploaded on video platforms like YouTube. This distributor attributed the decline in movie sales in the industry to the activities of satellite TV stations and illegal sharing of movies on pen drives. All distributors interviewed believed that the establishment of satellite TV stations in Tamale like Sagani TV and NTV has significantly affected sales in urban areas. Most urban viewers who have access to films on satellite TV have stopped buying movies for home viewing since they are screened regularly on TV.

When the satellite TV stations were first established, they approached industry stakeholders to secure permission to screen their old films on TV for free to help draw viewers to the stations. After they began screening the movies on TV, sales in urban areas dropped. Even after the TV stations found their feet, they did not open discussions about compensating filmmakers and producers for screening their movies. Although old movies are broadcast on these stations, the sale of new movies have been adversely affected. It was the hope of industry stakeholders that if old movies were screened, it would motivate audiences to come out and buy newly released movies. Many distributors believed that viewers are not motivated to purchase new movies when they can watch old movies on satellite TV.

Initially, the satellite TV stations promised to play advertisements of new movies on their channels in exchange for screening old movies. However, distributors say that the TV stations have not held up their end of the bargain since they asked them to pay for advertising after some time. As far as DVD patronage is concerned, women have been identified as the key demographic whose support promotes movie sales. Women viewers purchased more movies because they found the topics explored in the video films relatable. For example, movies that discussed the affairs of the household, life in polygynous households, marriage, and romantic and familial relationships, among others, were popular with women viewers. CCCs conducted with women viewers supported this observation made by distributors: "The women mostly buy films about family issues. When it comes to those films the ladies will just buy more than the men, but they are competing with the men in buying other films but when it's about family affairs, the women will buy the most. Usually, women prefer films about women" (Adiya Saani, Walma Productions, personal communication, 2018). The major reason for women's high consumption of Dagbanli movies was attributed to raising children. All distributors interviewed said that women bought DVDs to manage the social lives of their children. According to them, a woman would buy movies so that she could get her children to stay at home and not go out to loiter and get themselves in trouble. Other interlocutors observed that children pressured their mothers, who in turn bought the movies or pressured their husbands to buy them to keep the children from loitering. Some women made sure to stock up on DVDs in their households to keep their children at home and to make sure that they were not mistreated if they went to watch movies in the homes of neighbors. Other distributors believed that even when men came to their shops to buy movies, they were usually sent by their wives: "Mostly women buy more. Because when a man gets into the habit of buying movies, he is sent by his wife. The reason why the women make their husbands buy them is the kids" (Inusah Sayibu aka Abinchi, Nasara Productions, personal communication, 2018). Ultimately, a variety of reasons were presented to explain why women and villagers were the core viewership population who supported movie sales. This observation is in line with research in various communities across the world that have identified women as a key demographic in entertainment media viewing cultures. Villagers continued to patronize the movies because of the technology they had readily available for viewing. Women were found to be an integral part of the audience population because of the ways that they could relate to the films and how they could use them to control the social behavior of their children.

Radio 10,000: A Reimagining of the Mobile Cinema Van

As discussed earlier, the mobile cinema van has built the foundation for film distribution in many African communities. It preceded the growth of many national and regional film industries across the continent. I draw attention here to the current iteration and reimagining of the mobile cinema van by one man who is an integral part of the media distribution landscape and has operated for decades in Tamale and villages across the region. The current "Information Services Department evolved from an organisation established in the later part of 1939 as a branch of the Colonial Government Secretariat dedicated to convey[ing] news on the 2nd World War to the people of Gold Coast" (Information Services Department, 2020). Today the ISD develops public education campaigns, provides accreditation to the press for government events, and archives national events through photographs, among other activities.

The man who reimagined the colonial cinema van is Mohammed Fuseini, popularly known as Radio 10,000. This is the story of the cover of the book. According to Mohammed Fuseini, he has worked in the Northern Region's media industry since 1985. He started as a vendor of audio cassettes, VHS tapes, and later music CDs and DVDs. Radio 10,000 was a media distributor before the establishment of the Dagbanli movie industry. He worked with other media distributors like Kwabena Acheampong (popularly known as IK) of IK

Photos and worked closely with Dagbanli musicians in the production of their music. He is arguably the most popular vendor in the history of the industry. He started his career by selling media on foot, later bought a bicycle with which he would travel to villages to sell media, and then upgraded to the mobile van. Although his car is a jeep, I refer to it as a van because it was modeled after the colonial mobile cinema van. Although Radio 10,000 is widely known for his work in distribution, he has done some film editing and directing. Like many others, he is a self-taught distributor, editor, and director. Here, I discuss the peculiarity of Mohammed Fuseini's distribution style, the marketing strategies he employs in distributing media (specifically films), and other perspectives he has on the industry. Radio 10,000's vehicle is a familiar sight for people living in Tamale and its environs. It is usually sighted on Tamale market days.

At the beginning of his career, Mohammed Fuseini sold audio cassettes, which carried music by Peter Tosh, Don Williams, Kenny Rogers, Sonya Spence, and Bob Marley. Indian music was also widely purchased from his van. His vehicle mirrored the information van popular in colonial and postcolonial Ghana. The information van in many colonized African nations was used to disseminate information and push the colonialist state's ideology. "Correct! It looks like their [Information Services Department] van, but it has more baggage than their vans. Their vans can't carry many things. If they carry this many things they will not move. You know the vans are government-owned. As you see the machines on the van, nothing can fall from it. If it doesn't fall with the van itself, it won't fall at all. There are 5 TVs on the van" (Mohammed Fuseini, personal communication, 2018). He knew the strength and capacity of his van and was confident in its ability to carry all the weight mounted on it. According to Radio 10,000, he built his van into what it is today. He is a self-taught engineer. He does not believe that anyone can successfully replicate his vehicle:

> See it looks very unique. If you see it at night you will love it. Everything in
> it is useful. I have cameras in there that are still in good shape. I can go to an
> occasion and then I will shoot videos and put them in my computer. I actually
> don't have much education. I have a generator, battery . . . I made all of that
> myself. That's why no one can replicate this. Even the welders, I have to show
> them what to do if they need to fix it. If you go to a welder and ask them to
> make a car like Radio 10,000's they can't because they don't know how to.
> I own my knowledge. I have my metals and technical know-how. The welder
> will hold the welding gun and then I'll show him weld here and there. I spend
> quite a bit of money on it. That's why I can use it to support my family.
> (Mohammed Fuseini, personal communication, 2018)

FIGURE 9   Side view of Radio 10,000's van. (Photo by Kwame Acheampong, 2018.)

These information vans carried film screening equipment so that they could screen films for audiences in rural areas. He decorated his vehicle, an old blue Mitsubishi jeep, with colorful lights that lit up at night. Analog televisions were mounted on all sides of the top of the van. (See figures 9 and 10.)

Radio 10,000 went from village to village to screen movies to spark the interest of audiences to buy the DVDs that he had in stock. This distributor announced his presence by playing catchy music when the vehicle was in motion. When he selected a location to stop and conduct sales, he would screen various movies for the viewing of prospective customers. He has been working in the media industry before radio and satellite TV stations were established in the Northern Region. When I asked how he came up with his name, he said that the name references the economic model of radio. According to him, all radio channels in the region are freely accessed through radio sets, but when he started his work he provided media content at a fee. He believed that when customers bought media from him they paid him, unlike radio stations, which were not directly paid by audiences. That he was paid by media audiences for media consumption made him stand out:

> You know we have many radio stations now in Tamale. We have Fiila FM, Justice FM, North Star, Zaa Radio, Radio Savannah, Radio Tamale, so many of them. When you do your work, you should have a unique name that people associate with you. So, all the radio stations I mentioned are free for listeners.

FIGURE 10 Inside Radio 10,000's van. (Photo by Kwame Acheampong, 2018.)

You don't pay for it. If you have a radio set you can tune in. But with my radio, you have to pay to be able to tune in to my station. That's why there is money involved. Radio 10,000 means you have to pay to be able to tune in to my station. If you observe, you will realize that my radio station is mobile with the business that I do. But you have to pay before you can tune in to my station. (Mohammed Fuseini, personal communication, 2018)

Radio 10,000 is known to make strategic stops at the busiest locations in the central business district of Tamale. When he is not making rounds in the city, he is moving from village to village to sell all types of media (audio cassettes, DVDs, music, and film). Interestingly, I found that the public could "tune in" to this "radio station" without necessarily paying for it. The whole point of this marketing model was to draw in customers. Therefore, people within the vicinity of the van could enjoy the music and movies without paying for it. However, this vendor made an important point about the instant sales that he could make from playing and screening media content when he made his rounds. He still travels to the villages he used to go to when he ran his business on a bicycle. According to him, he is a self-taught film producer, editor, and distributor:

I don't have formal education, but I am an intelligent person. Now the Dagbanli movies that I produce, I edit my own films even though I have no formal education. I do everything on my own and bring them out to sell. I pay attention and observe a lot. Once I am able to watch and observe something, I can do it on my own. Those places, I used to ride bicycles there. I used to go to Gushayu market day, Yendi market day, Katiŋ market day (Tolon District), Kumbuŋ market day, Savelugu market day. When I was using a bicycle, I used to go to all these places. With my own car, I still go the same routes. (Mohammed Fuseini, personal communication, 2018)

He often plans his sales rounds to overlap with the market day at the villages where he sells movies. Just like for vendors who worked with distributors, market days are the peak sales day for this distributor. On market days, customers would get ready for Radio 10,000 and wait at the locations where he made his stops. Like distributors who manage stores, he screens movies on his van to get the attention of customers. Unlike distributors who may place advertisements on radio and TV, his van is his marketing tool, the loudspeakers that play music and films are his marketing tools. According to him, this marketing strategy has worked for him since he started the business of movie distribution: "So, in the car, I have everything. I will screen the film for free to advertise it and then people will watch and feel like buying. It was a business strategy so that they would buy. When I go to the market, many customers come to buy from me. I'll play a movie and then after it's done, I'll take it out and play another one. Instead of trying to convince them by word of mouth on what movie to buy, I just screen the film and they decide on what they want to buy" (Mohammed Fuseini, personal communication, 2018). Beyond screening entire films on the TVs mounted on the van, Radio 10,000 believes that being a trustworthy and honest person while running his business attracts customers to him. (See figure 11.)

Some customers would purchase the movie they had just watched on the van so that their friends and family could watch it too. Others asked for movies in the same genre after watching a movie mounted on the van. Although Radio 10,000 had hopes that the video film industry had the potential to grow, he identified some of the challenges facing the industry that needed to be addressed. He pointed out that poor video quality was one of the major factors mitigating the growth of the industry: "You meet to educate each other on techniques of shooting scenes. The person doing the editing should also spend a lot of time and attention on it. There are a lot of DVDs that are on good films, but bad editing make them virtually unsellable. Some don't have enough experience to work independently as producers or camera operators etc." (Mohammed Fuseini, personal communication, 2018). This challenge has been identified by industry stakeholders as one of the issues facing the distribution sector.

Radio 10,000 has contributed significantly to the growth of distribution in the movie industry. His insights on the evolution of distribution, his intricate

FIGURE 11 Front view of Radio 10,000's van. (Photo by Kwame Acheampong, 2018.)

knowledge of distribution dynamics, and his unique distribution style nuance the complexities of distribution and demonstrate the trajectory the movie industry may take in supporting the growth and development of film distribution.

Viewing Cultures, from Video Centers to Netflix

In this chapter we have learned that there is tremendous work to be done in knowledge production on Indigenous-language media in many African communities. While I mapped the history of Dagbanli movie distribution in Ghana to show the complexities of global media distribution hegemonies, I highlighted the intricacies and complexities of video distribution in this region and beyond, demonstrating the way that the industry is situated in global, continental, and national film hierarchies. I demonstrated that despite the challenges faced by these Indigenous-language film industries, stakeholders have employed innovative strategies to sustain the industry while positioning it as a site of resistance. The industry is doing this while serving communities who are often excluded from media representations nationally and globally.

Even though cinema going was popular among Ghanaians for some time, several factors mitigated the growth of cinema culture, some of which were political and others economic. Politically, coups d'état, which were accompanied by curfews and restrictions in movement, negatively affected cinema culture in Ghana (Meyer, 2015). As cinema culture died off, cinema halls in Southern Ghana were sold to churches (which used them for church services and other meetings), ultimately mitigating cinema-going culture in the country (Aveh, 2010). In Northern Ghana, however, cinema halls like Victory and Rivoli were eventually sold or rented out to businesses that used them as megastores or warehouses as of June 2023.

Distributors in Ghallywood found that selling video films to take home could help address the issue of piracy that had increasingly become the bane of the industry, and this picked up in other industries in Tamale and Kumasi. These challenges in distribution coupled with other contextual factors that constrained cinema-going culture led to the development of film distribution networks via VHS tapes, video CDs, DVDs, and others. For a spell in the 1990s, IK Photos together with Ahmed Adam and others worked on Dagbanli movie distribution via VHS tapes. Similarly, movies to take home via DVDs is the major medium of distribution in the Dagbanli movie industry today.

Although piracy is one of the main challenges plaguing film industries across the continent, market choking and saturation of the movie market has been identified by stakeholders as a major problem mitigating the growth of the industry. According to distributors, this problem can be attributed to the tendency of filmmakers and producers to rush movies onto the market before they are ready and the lax regulations guiding the production and release of movies.

Although new media and streaming platforms have been estimated to revolutionize film distribution on the continent, for many Indigenous-language filmmakers who are affected by the digital divide, these platforms have been counterproductive since digital pirates have used platforms like YouTube to illegally share their content and profit from it. It is imperative therefore to contextualize how new media and streaming platforms support the marginalization of distribution networks in these communities, highlighting the way that they impact video film distribution. While Netflix is gaining ground in markets like

Nigeria and South Africa, it is important to understand this expansion within global media hegemonies where English-language media is privileged over French-, Arabic-, Portuguese-, and Indigenous-language media on the continent and beyond. In addition, how do Indigenous-language media economies grapple with issues of media and cultural imperialism while working to find more effective national, continental, and global distribution platforms.

Ultimately, Dagbanli movie distribution has evolved significantly from video centers at a time when filmmakers did not have access to screen video films at theaters to DVDs that are sold to take home for viewing. Movie marketing has taken ingenious forms with changing technology, even though radio and TV still occupy important positions in publicity and marketing. Piracy and market choking are some of the major challenges facing the industry today. Piracy took the form of pirating DVDs for sale and digital piracy via YouTube and illegal sharing of movies using pen drives. Despite all these challenges, the industry has come to establish itself as a site of resistance and liberation for Dagbanli speakers who rarely see themselves represented on TV channels with nationwide coverage such as Ghana Television (GTV).

6

Television for
Social Change

●●●●●●●●●●●●●●●●●●●●●●

Sagani ku tooi kari saa, naɣila
saa n pun je mibu

Television occupies an important position not just in the Ghanaian mediascape but in the African media landscape. While radio remains the medium of the masses and the most accessible media platform for many Africans, accessibility to television in its various forms is seeing an uptick. The medium has grown from a platform that was limited to elite consumption from the 1960s to the 1980s to a space that the masses are all too familiar with. Nigeria was the first country in Africa to establish television broadcasting in 1959 (Nwulu et al., 2010). And many countries followed suit in the 1960s. Ghana joined the television wave in 1965. For a while, television was the medium of the privileged class because TV sets were significantly more expensive than radio sets and required power to operate in ways that radio did not since many communities were connected to the radioscape even though they were not connected to electricity. These connections were facilitated by batteries or solar power.

Today, television has tremendously evolved not just in Ghana but across the continent, drawing attention to the importance of understanding this medium within global conversations on digital television, satellite television, streaming television, and others. In this chapter, I discuss the history of television in Ghana, connecting it to issues of accessibility and then grounding the discussion in the current digital media landscape and how that is shaping this medium.

The history of television in Ghana cannot be disconnected from Ghana's colonial legacies that have shaped what has become the major language of mediation, English. Whereas television took off in Ghana in 1965, it wasn't until 1997 that private commercial TV stations began to join the media scene following a liberalization of the airwaves. The lateness of commercial television to the scene can be attributed to the monopoly that the public broadcaster, Ghana Broadcasting Corporation (GBC), had over the media landscape for decades. The series of coups d'état that the country was subjected to between the 1960s and the 1980s also contributed to a stifling of the growth of the media landscape. Today there are so many media organizations in the country across the television and radio spaces that they are in competition with one another to generate revenue from a relatively small market. Although media liberalization in the 1990s opened up the Ghanaian public sphere and provided English-language television programs, a close observation of their operations demonstrates that they do not provide a variety of programming to address audience needs. That they provide variety in content does not necessarily mean that content produced by these media organizations effectively challenges dominant ideology in the Ghanaian public sphere. While I provide the historical context for television in the country, I am particularly concerned with the work of Indigenous-language TV stations that have seen an explosion since the mediascape began to adopt satellite TV and digital terrestrial free-to-air TV.

Here, I contribute to scholarly conversations in media studies by deconstructing Indigenous-language television, which has largely been understudied. I center the perspectives of marginalized communities while opening avenues to reconceptualize contemporary media within African contexts to rewrite history. My focus on the work of Indigenous-language television stations not only draws attention to audience communities that have historically been erased from media representation but also demonstrates the way that these stations ground their content-creation process in Indigenous knowledge systems and values that community members hold dear. I not only discuss the way that these media organizations construct their work as a site of cultural affirmation and education but also provide a critique on how they can operate to disrupt marginalization with regard to gender, religion, ethnicity, and so on.

Television Histories

Even though Ghana Television (GTV) began transmission in 1965, it wasn't until 1985 that Ghanaians had access to color television (Alhassan, 2005). Again, global media histories demonstrate the marginalization of Africa in the global mediascape by showing us how media innovations diffused across the continent. Within Ghana, the North is subjected to a double bind of this marginalization because it is often the last part of the country that these innovations reach. So even though GTV was broadcasting from the 1960s, it wasn't until 1989 that one of Northern Ghana's largest cities was connected to the national electricity grid. Following the connection of the North to electricity, television access began to grow with well-to-do citizenry purchasing TV sets to catch GTV broadcasts. The diffusion of this innovation was still in its novel stages since only a small number of people could afford color TV sets. This meant that communal television viewing was quite widespread where owners of TV sets would bring them out at night into the compound for community members to watch. During the day, it was not uncommon to see children stand behind the windows of their neighbors' rooms to watch TV. Throughout the 1990s, GTV held a monopoly in the television space in the North.

It wasn't until the mid- to late 1990s that television ownership became widespread in Tamale and the Northern Region by extension. According to Fadi Fattal, group director of Max Media Group, Metro TV extended operational coverage to other major cities such as Sunyani, Tamale, Bolgatanga, and Ho in April 2004 (personal communication, December 18, 2023). Metro TV thus became the first private commercial TV station to extend coverage to the Northern Region. This extension of coverage took place seven years after the establishment of private commercial TV in the country. This means that for more than a decade since TV innovations were diffused to the North, viewers were limited to only one channel on the analog platform. To understand the current Ghanaian TV landscape, we need to go back into the country's media histories to deconstruct the vision of its foremothers as far as public media broadcasting is concerned.

Nowhere is the historical and current mandate of GTV and by extension the GBC articulated more clearly than in the speech of Dr. Kwame Nkrumah (1965, p. 3) at the inauguration of the Ghana Television Service: "Ghana's Television will be used to supplement our educational programme and foster a lively interest in the world around us. It will not cater for cheap entertainment nor commercialism. Its paramount object will be education in the broadest and purest sense. Television must assist in the socialist transformation of Ghana." Here, President Nkrumah reiterates the importance of education as the guiding principle for the mission and vision of the GBC. In his vision, education included promoting and making science and technical training accessible to the masses, centering topics on agriculture and providing general information on vocational work and practical skills for people at home and at school. The GBC at its onset sought to foster national unity and integration due to the highly multicultural nature of the newly independent Ghana. The public broadcaster reflected Ghanaian culture by broadcasting in select languages across the various cultural zones of the country. According to Alhassan (2005), the public broadcaster's conceptualization of national integration was conflated with homogenization of ideological thinking, which meant that

GBC's monopoly over the airwaves did not often make room for dissenting perspectives to be heard in the Ghanaian public sphere. I argue that with a liberalization of the mediascape today, very little room has been made for dissenting perspectives or perspectives that challenge dominant ideology in the country to be meaningfully engaged. Indeed, while the existence of privately owned commercial television stations means that Ghanaians have a variety of choices to pick from for television programming, these TV stations are not necessarily disrupting the status quo. The various media organizations across newspaper, television, and radio present identical perspectives on various topics in the country with the exception of a few. It is imperative to note that there are remnants of Nkrumah's vision of media for social change with an emphasis on educating the citizenry. I discuss this later when I delve into the work of African-language television stations in the country.

According to Melkote and Steeves (2015), development communication is concerned with using media and communication technologies to bring about social change in local communities while centering the agency and self-determination of community members to drive social justice efforts. In this vein, the state broadcaster has utilized their national platform to provide education on health and agriculture among others. In addition, following the establishment of GBC-TV in 1965, English literacy programs were introduced and school telecasting was also introduced where the use of television in classrooms was promoted (Amoh, 2022). Key among the highlights of bringing television to the masses was developing and actualizing the concept of community viewing centers where TV was brought to the masses, especially for people who could not afford to purchase TV sets (Amoh, 2022). Although this development was a result of the socialist vision that shaped the activities of broadcasting in Ghana, it is a great example of development communication in action where the state took it upon itself to make TV content more accessible to these marginalized communities. It is imperative to note that although these community viewing centers were widely embraced by the masses, they seemed to focus their operations on Southern cities like Accra, Takoradi, Cape Coast, and Koforidua (Amoh, 2022) while the Northern half was largely left out, again indicating the double oppression that the North has historically and is presently being subjected to. According to Alhaji Adam Cockra (personal communication, November 27, 2023), a veteran journalist from Tamale who worked at GBC for forty-two years from 1966 to 2008, when the North eventually became a part of the television broadcast landscape, "a small transmitter was installed in Tamale to take care of the North. Staff in Tamale received by Ghana Airways [flight] what was telecast the previous day in Accra. . . . In other words, everything viewers in the North saw on TV was a day old. Even then, only Tamale and its environs could view TV until the 1990s." Despite these structural hurdles in bringing television to Ghanaians marginalized based on geographical location, ethnicity, and class, President Nkrumah's (1965, p. 5) vision for media in Ghana went beyond education and into the realm of consciousness raising: "Our broadcasting service should struggle ceaselessly to make itself the people's service. It should identify itself fully with the people's aspirations for a fuller life. It should continue to fight uncompromisingly against the forces militating against our progress. It will be its task to expose and unmask imperialism, colonialism and neocolonialism in all its forms and manifestations, and support our endeavors for the political unification of our Continent." While this statement was made at the time when African countries were fighting for liberation from colonial rule and the African diaspora in America was fighting for civil liberties, this statement is still relevant today in a moment when the Global South is subjected to the violence of neocolonialism and imperialism from Europe and North America. In recent times, however, the media environment in the country has shifted heavily toward commercialization and privilege profit over the ideology being communicated by the content transmitted on television and radio. In an internet age, an uber liberalization of the media space means that there is a level of saturation that forces commercial television stations to prioritize profit over social justice and liberation.

In fact, media organizations and media watchdog organizations have slacked on this mandate and have become stooges not just of the ruling elite but of imperialist core nations such as France and the United States, thereby departing heavily from Nkrumah's vision for media in the country. For example, the French ambassador to Ghana from 2018 to 2022, Anne Sophie Avé, hosted a program called *Touch of France* that was broadcast on GHOne TV and Metro TV (private commercial stations) from 2019 to 2021 where French propaganda and soft power were promoted under the guise of cultural exchange, a development that Nkrumah would describe as a neocolonization of the media landscape. Also, the U.S. embassy was a major sponsor for the twenty-seventh Ghana Journalists Awards, held in October 2023 in Accra. It is therefore no surprise that journalism in the country today has failed to interrogate and critically challenge U.S. imperialism in the country where, for example, the American military has established a military base and its soldiers have more rights than Ghanaian citizens (Prashad, 2022). Not only is the media failing to do its watchdog role by not interrogating American imperialism, but they are also not asking the right questions to inform the public about the implications of these developments on the sovereignty of Ghana as a nation. In addition, the embassies of Global North nations in Europe and North America occupy an integral position in the civil society circles of the country by funding research, organizing and funding journalism training workshops, wining and dining the movers and shakers in the media and journalism, and so on, which can often stifle journalists' ability to more sharply critique the colonial and imperialist actions of these nations. These interferences coupled with a largely colonial educational curriculum maintain the status quo and even protect the interests of these supposed "benefactor" nations. Therefore, understanding the current state of television in the country cannot be divorced from the values that constructed the introduction of TV to the public in the 1960s.

The television histories of the country are incomplete without highlighting the role that women played in developing the medium. Due to the Pan-African values espoused in Nkrumah's vision for media in a newly independent Ghana, key aspects of television development were shaped by Pan-Africanists like Shirley Graham Du Bois from the United States and Genoveva Marais from South Africa. Marais served as director of programs for the television service at its inception, introducing and shaping programming toward the Pan-African and socialist vision upon which the foundation of the GBC was built (Amoh, 2022). According to Blaylock (2022), the development of TV programming targeted at women produced colonial logics of gender and reinforced middle-class values. Graham Du Bois, in her work as director of television, made strong connections between media and African Indigenous knowledges around communication such as the talking drum and griot culture (Blaylock, 2022). This connection is the foundation for the argument I make in this book about not only Africanizing media and communications but writing into our histories the strong connections between Indigenous media and communication practices and contemporary television. Despite women's early contributions to the development of television in Ghana, there are very few women in management positions in television stations today. Gender representation on television has wildly departed from the Pan-African, anticolonial values that underpinned the early days of TV development. The male gaze dominates television representations, and media narratives on gender are often filtered through a lens of objectification and other gender tropes that are maintained by patriarchal systems.

Africanizing Television Today

According to the National Communications Authority (2023), there are 170 authorized TV stations in Ghana, and of the 170 about 118 are on air as of 2023. This is more than double the number of TV stations that were on air in 2016. Majority of these stations transmit through digital terrestrial free-to-air TV or satellite television broadcasting (National Communications Authority, 2023). Even though GTV had a monopoly on the television space from 1965 until the early 1990s, there are many television stations today transmitting across various platforms. While early commercial privately owned TV stations like Metro TV and TV3 provided broadcasts predominantly in English, newer

TV stations that have been around since the 2010s have focused programming on Ghanaian languages like Akan, Dagbanli, Ewe, and others. These stations are filling a linguistic gap in the media landscape that for a long time only radio was able to address.

To understand the importance of language in decolonizing the mediascape specifically television, I turn to Ghanaian language TV stations using the Northern Region as a focus. I argue that although Indigenous-language TV stations fill the gap that many English stations are unable to address by communicating to audiences in their languages, thereby affirming them, there is more room for improvement since these stations can be prone to reproducing colonial logics in the way that they represent gender and religion. I assert that these stations are strategically positioned to realize the development communication goals upon which the country's media space was founded. By turning attention to NTV, Sagani TV, and Zaa TV, we are able to deconstruct the civic and cultural role of television while understanding the potential these stations hold to bring about targeted systemic change in one of Ghana's poorest regions. By paying attention to the topics covered by the programs of these stations, we are challenged to value the contributions of Indigenous-language media to safeguarding Ghanaian languages from linguicide while instilling in the citizenry a sense of cultural pride and belonging.

NTV was established in 2015, Sagani TV in 2017, Zaa TV in 2021. Before these stations, Discovery TV was established in 2013 by Philip Assibit Akpeena and went off air not long thereafter. Since NTV, Sagani TV, and Zaa TV have been a part of the television space in Ghana, they have contributed to highlighting the narratives of communities in the Northern half of the country who were for decades merely spectators in the media space centered on Accra. Today people in the Northern Region and beyond can turn on television and hear languages such as Dagbanli, Mampruli, and a few others. Although major private stations such as TV3, Metro TV, Citi TV, GHOne TV, Joy Prime TV, and others pursue the commercial bottom line in their programing that targets predominantly English speakers, television stations in the Northern Region focus more on centering community needs in programming. I assert that the work of satellite TV stations in Tamale is influenced by development communication values and Nkrumah's vision of the importance of centering African identities and communal values on television in the country. Although TV stations in Tamale may not necessarily be directly influenced by Nkrumahist ideologies, they have been influenced by the tone set by the first radio station in the Northern Region, Radio Savannah. As we learned earlier, Radio Savannah is a GBC radio station whose operations were explicitly shaped by GBC values focused on promoting development. GBC's mission statement is "to lead the broadcasting and communications industry through quality programming which promotes the development and cultural aspirations of Ghana" (GBC, n.d.). Similarly, the notion of development was at the core of the mission and vision statements of each of the three television stations. While NTV and Sagani TV both mention "development" a couple of times in their statements, Zaa TV mentions "social change." According to Melkote and Steeves (2015), development and social change go hand in hand. Sagani TV specifically identifies the structural marginalization of the North in their mission statement and aims "to help bridge the development gap between Southern and Northern Ghana" (Sagani TV, n.d.). Zaa TV also espouses a development communication praxis by working "to provide public awareness, civil education and advocate progressive social change among various communities in Northern Region and Ghana in general" (Zaa TV, n.d.). In efforts to Africanize Ghana television, the Graham Du Bois–led GBC-TV sought to bring television to the masses by either transmitting some content in Ghanaian languages or utilizing translators to translate English content in the various community viewing centers across major Southern cities (Amoh, 2022). Many contemporary TV stations have revolutionized this notion of Africanization by transmitting over 70 percent of their broadcasts in Ghanaian languages. NTV's slogan, "the station that speaks your language," strongly articulates this value of Africanization. I read this slogan in the literal sense to mean a station that speaks Dagbanli and Mampruli. I also deconstruct its metaphorical meaning by paying attention to the way that NTV curates content to address issues affecting the people of and from the North who are their core audience. This praxis of contemporary television to center the language and cultures of the communities they serve in the face of imperialism and neocolonialism is in the spirit of the vision that Graham Du Bois, Marais, and Nkrumah had for television in the 1960s.

Ultimately, I assert that development communication as a theoretical and praxis framework overlaps and aligns with socialist television as conceptualized by Nkrumah because these concepts value egalitarianism, communality, community self-determination, and social justice. At the core of socialist television are the values of equality, humanism, and education that are grounded in audience participation (Huxtable, 2018). As we parse out the impact of television on Africans and Ghanaians, it is important to contextualize these developments within the notion of the digital divide since certain working-class sections of the audience communities are excluded from these developments due to their lack of access to the tools to connect to digital or satellite TV. Next, we take a close look at the work of NTV, Sagani TV, and Zaa TV to deconstruct the way that they operate as commercial TV stations while trying to stay true to their commitment to center audience needs in their broadcasts.

Cultural Education on Television

Although platforms like radio at the onset developed content to provide cultural education for audiences in Ghanaian languages, television today is leading a cultural revolution in not only centering Ghanaian languages but explicitly articulating a praxis rooted in cultural preservation, affirmation, and education. At the center of this praxis is language and the importance of preserving the essence of African languages. Although commercial TV stations like TV3 provide cultural programming such as *Ghana's Most Beautiful (GMB)* that is widely popular with the masses, these programs are limited in reach because they mostly transmit in English to reach a wider national audience (Dennis, 2018). Contestants of *GMB* therefore often resort to code-switching between English and their Indigenous language in order to reach a wider audience, with the majority of their performance being in English. This means that this type of cultural programming with wide national appeal superficially engages with Ghanaian languages. Regional TV stations that transmit mainly in Indigenous languages do not have to deal with the burden of reaching a national audience and therefore are able to provide programming that deeply engages cultural discourses in the language of their communities of operation.

On TV and radio, there is very little tolerance of code-switching especially in the Northern Region, where any linguistic code-switching is read as a lack of proficiency in the Ghanaian language and a disregard for upholding cultural autonomy and a lack of cultural pride. In other African contexts like South Africa, which is multiethnic like West African communities and also multiracial (in ways that many West African countries are not), linguistic code-switching is highly embraced and constitutes the normative language structure of the television landscape (Barnard, 2006). In Ghana and Burkina Faso, however, linguistic code-switching is read as a legacy of colonization and a disrespect to upholding the cultures of the community. According to Ouédraogo (2007), on the Burkinabè television program *Tales of the Lagle Naaba*, which has been running since the 1960s, storytellers and performers endeavor to speak exclusively in the Mooré language and wear Moose/Mossi cultural clothing. This observation is in alignment with the praxis of TV stations transmitting in Dagbanli where the language and culture are centered in programs dedicated to cultural education.

While the programming on NTV, Sagani TV, and Zaa TV focuses on amplifying Dagbaŋ cultures, they also do the important work of cultural education, preservation, and affirmation. For example, in the early years of NTV, programs like *Duduhugu* (meaning "kitchen") brought audiences closer to Indigenous Dagbaŋ gastronomy by demonstrating how certain meals were prepared, meals and recipes that are being structurally erased from the community because of cultural imperialism and food colonization masked as globalization and modernization. This program was educational for children and adults alike and brought Indigenous knowledges around gastronomy closer to community members. Cultural education on television through Ghanaian languages not only supports the preservation of Ghanaian cultures but also serves to shape positive attitudes toward these cultures threatened by imperialism (Dennis, 2018). The work of Indigenous-language television stations in cultural affirmation, preservation, and education echoes Nkrumah's sentiments about the key role of television in promoting African cultural autonomy: "Our Television Service should be African in its outlook; and in its content, even though it may express and reflect outside and foreign experiences, should remain geared to the needs of Ghana and Africa" (Nkrumah, 1965, p. 3). In the area of cultural preservation, work is being done at home and in diasporic communities to maintain Ghanaian cultural autonomy. TV stations are recording and broadcasting cultural events such as the Damba and Buɣum festivals, funerals of chiefs, and chieftaincy enskinment ceremonies so that community members at home and abroad can stay connected to the community. Between 2021 and 2023, Zaa TV telecast video recordings of the celebrations of the Damba festival by the Dagbaŋ and Northern diaspora in American cities like Atlanta and Jersey City. In this vein, not only is Dagbaŋ culture exported to the diaspora, but diasporic cultural celebrations are also brought back home for the community to engage with. Here is what the CEO of NTV had to say about the work they do to preserve the culture: "When it is Damba festival, we show it live from Yendi and it is all over the country and people who are down South as Dagombas [Dagbamba] they see what is happening on Damba day. Yeah, so that is how to preserve the culture" (personal communication, Alhaji Adam Cockra, NTV CEO, March 2023). These stations reach the diaspora across Ghana and the rest of the world through satellite broadcasting and social media. This means that some of the programming caters to the needs of diaspora communities. In my conversation with the manager of Zaa TV, Yahaya Mubarik, I found not only that these cultural programs promote cultural education and affirmation but that they are also sites of cultural revival that inspire feelings of nostalgia in community members. For example, through the *Simpa Dance Competition* many young children who have never witnessed the simpa dance get a chance to learn about this dance culture. For older people who grew up participating in these dances, the program sparks feelings of nostalgia, a sense of cultural pride, and deep connections to their cultural heritage.

In the current television landscape, there is a media convergence happening that we aren't seeing strongly in the work of English-language TV stations based in Accra. Stations like NTV, Sagani TV, and Zaa TV either broadcast programs on Facebook Live or upload the recorded programs on YouTube.

Sagani TV uploads the recordings of programs such as *Kavini* on YouTube to reach a wider mostly diaspora audience. The convergence of television and social media in a way addresses some of the issues of accessibility that exclude certain community members from accessing these programs. For community members who cannot afford to purchase the technologies needed to connect to satellite TV, they can join on Facebook (which may be more accessible) and participate as audiences. Many of the programs on the stations allow for audience participation through phoning in, texting, or posting comments on the Facebook livestream of the program.

Beyond audience participation, we need to closely examine selected TV programs and their impact on promoting cultural education. The programs broadcast on Dagbanli TV stations not only provide cultural education but specifically improve the linguistic proficiency of community members. Many diaspora communities abroad especially watch these programs to not only stay grounded in their culture but also maintain and improve their proficiency in the language. Stations like Sagani TV understand the importance of cultural education via language education and take actionable steps to stand out in their work toward these efforts. While many stations broadcast in Dagbanli and display announcements, news headlines, and so forth on the news ticker at the bottom of the screen in English even though the major language of broadcast is Dagbanli, Sagani TV endeavors to do this work in Dagbanli: "We are now trying to encourage parents that advocacy of the mother tongue, the L1 [first language] being a foundation for every other language. Yes, you know, we are really trying to advocate for that. So I said, we need to start writing our headlines in Dagbanli to challenge the kids at home, to try to read their own" (personal communication, Ziblim David, Sagani TV manager, March 2023). The manager of Zaa TV understands the importance of providing cultural education to children while affirming their cultural identities. Here, Dagbanli TV stations promote Indigenous languages in the face of coloniality because many children are indoctrinated in schools to believe in the superiority of English over their own languages. In addition, programs like *Baŋsim Chuɣu* (Zaa TV) and *Kavini* (Sagani TV) specifically focus on amplifying the histories and knowledges of Dagbamba from past to present. *Kavini*, hosted by Ziblim David, is a weekly program involving a griot (drummer/praise singer) who comes in to provide cultural education on various topics such as Dagbaŋ philosophies, ceremonies, rites, and rituals. *Baŋsim Chuɣu*, hosted by a junior high school Dagbanli teacher, Nana Sibri, is a reality TV quiz show that tests participants on Dagbaŋ geography, language, history, and culture. Similar to the Burkinabè television program *Tales of the Lagle Naaba*, the storytelling program *Dagbaŋ Salma Dundoŋ* was introduced in 2023 on Zaa TV to share Dagbanli folktales with audiences. In this program, a storyteller regales audiences with didactic folktales about *kpatinariga* (the spider), *kunduŋ* (the hyena), *buu* (the goat), and others so that the public may be entertained and learn life lessons from them. Both programs bear similarities with GTV's popular storytelling program for children, *By the Fireside*, which was widely popular in the 1990s. Other programs such as *Gbewaa Bihi ni o Yaansi* (Zaa TV) that provide coverage on topics about Dagbaŋ royalty also bring cultural education about the chieftaincy institution to the masses. Programming centered on preserving culture and educating the masses about cultures and traditions that are at risk of being lost is important for strengthening the cultural identities of community members while providing education on the heritage of the community. NTV specifically articulates their commitment to this cause by centering indigeneity in their mission and vision statement. This is what part of the motto of the station as presented in the statement says: "NTV-touching lives, changing situations with Indigenous communication." Clearly articulating "Indigenous communication" as part of the praxis of the station demonstrates the values espoused by the station, values that align with Shirley Graham Du Bois's vision for GBC-TV to promote Indigenous communication. In my conversation with Ziblim David, I learned that many of these stations believe that it is their mandate to preserve and transmit Dagbaŋ cultures through the television medium: "People are getting to understand our customs, who we are, what makes us unique, you know, our rich culture" (personal communication, Ziblim David, Sagani TV manager, March 2023). This mandate of cultural education that television stations have taken on is a praxis rooted in resistance to colonization from both dominant cultures of the Ghanaian South and dominant cultures in the continental and global space. These stations are therefore disrupting the historical homogenization of the television space that was dominated by programming that catered mostly to English-speaking audiences while ignoring non-English-speaking audiences. This disruption is not just a resistance to cultural imperialism but more importantly an amplification of the silenced histories and narratives of communities that have historically been symbolically annihilated from the mediascape of the country. These stations' focus of cultural affirmation and education resulted in the consequence of resistance to coloniality. Beyond cultural education, these stations are cognizant of the harms perpetuated by certain cultural practices and endeavor to not platform or promote them on television, a development that has been observed on Burkina Faso's National Television where Moose/Mossi folktales are presented to the masses by cultural custodians (Ouédraogo, 2007).

Development Communication on Television

While many commercial TV stations located in the South of the country pursue a commercial imperative first of all as a major driving force in their programming, many TV stations in the Northern Region endeavor to balance the pursuit of the commercial imperative with promoting the rich cultural heritage of the region. Here, the media tradition that was established by GBC's Radio Savannah has tremendously shaped the values espoused by many of these TV stations; values that can be filtered through a socialist media and development communication analytical framework. Ironically, one of the major challenges of TV stations in the region is a challenge to stay sustainable since many are operating within a small market space and an increasingly saturated media space. Nevertheless, all three privately owned commercial TV stations support programming that promotes and preserves the diverse cultures of the region.

In examining the program lineup of the stations, watching the various programs on the channels and speaking with managers of the stations, all three stations work intentionally to re-right narratives about the North by disrupting harmful stereotypes and restoring dignity to the narrative imaginary of the community, its diaspora and the rest of the Ghanaian community. One of my key observations about the work being done in the broadcasts of these stations indicate that they have identified who their primary audience is and work on programming to satisfy the needs and gratifications of these audiences. Key among identifying the primary audience of these stations are the primary issues affecting the people of the North which are usually framed as developmental in nature. According to the Ghana Statistical Service (2022b, p. 27), "the Northern region has the highest number of persons who are multidimensionally poor and illiterate." Therefore, with high poverty rates, low literacy rates and low educational attainment rates, it is only proper that programs on these stations aim to address the needs of audiences who are affected by these structural issues. In my conversation with the founder and former CEO of NTV, Prince Siita Sofo in Accra, he said that the goal of "NTV basically is to bridge the development gap between Northern and Southern Ghana" (March, 2023). According to him, the goal of the station is to translate government policies into the language of the people for them to become a more civically engaged citizenry.

Therefore, a development communication praxis and orientation begins to emerge in not just the ideologies that guide the work of the stations but the very content that is broadcast to audiences. For example, agricultural programs are popular on these stations because farming is one of the major economic activities of the five regions of the North. Therefore, programs like *Pukparigu Saha* on Zaa TV provide farmer education from the time of sowing seeds to the period of harvest. Key among topics discussed on the program include the dangers of bush burning and wildfires, how to deal with invasive birds that descend on rice farms around the time of harvest, proper fertilizer application to ensure a good yield, where to purchase specific farm implements and products, and so forth. Programs like these are often sponsored by agribusinesses

or NGOs dedicated to agriculture. Experts such as agricultural extension offi-
cers share their knowledge with farmers, who often get the chance to directly
interact with them during the phone-in session. Although these stations consider themselves to be commercial TV stations like their counterparts in Accra,
they understand their unique positioning to address the developmental issues
of their communities through the content they broadcast. Alhaji Adam Cockra
clearly articulates what these stations believe their mandate to be to their audiences: "And we also do programs on agriculture called 'post-harvest losses.'
These are programs that will benefit the people instead of also trying to be like
TV3 or Joy FM or some TV station elsewhere" (Alhaji Adam Cockra, NTV
CEO, March 2023). Stations like Sagani TV on their *Nuu ni Baŋsim* program
bring the intricacies of vocational and technical education to their publics. This
program parallels the goals that Dr. Nkrumah had for Ghanaian socialist
television, which included highlighting the importance of technical and vocational education and training. Other stakeholders in the TV space emphasized
the responsibility of the press to safeguard the peace that the region is currently
enjoying given that several communities in the country have struggled with
chieftaincy and ethnic conflicts in the past.

Beyond agricultural programming, many of the stations discuss current
affairs on their morning shows and have standalone current affairs programs,
many of which involve going into rural communities to speak to community
members about the developmental challenges plaguing these communities.
Very often, community members directly call on their representatives to address
the urgent needs of the community, some of which include lack of access to
potable water, terrible roads, lack of health, and school facilities, among others.
Here, the media in the region not only play their watchdog role but serve as a
conduit between the everyday people and their representatives who serve in par-
liament or at the district level. These direct appeals are often broadcast on the
news bulletins of these stations to bring attention to the pressing needs of communities that would otherwise not get the attention of big media organizations
in Accra. Leading up to the district assembly elections on December 19, 2023,
several TV stations provided extensive education to voters so that they could
cast a valid ballot. According to the Ghana Statistical Service (2022b), the
Northern Region has the largest illiterate population of all the regions in the
country. This means that some voters often do not have access to knowledge
about how to cast a valid ballot. Therefore, education on these issues is paramount in ensuring that the citizenry cast valid ballots that count. For example, on one of the stations, Abdulai Ayaala, the deputy regional director for the
National Commission for Civic Education in the Northern Region, was invited
to provide education on the elections. Other stations used the election period
to bring attention to the lack of women representation in partisan politics at
the district, regional, and national levels. Some of the programs challenged

patriarchal ideas about women in politics and disrupted harmful notions about the unelectability of women candidates.

In addition to holding leaders accountable for their work or lack thereof in local communities, TV stations are increasingly becoming sources for crowd-funding for poor people to raise funds to pay for healthcare costs. It has become common for TV stations to take on the plight of people with diseases such as cancer, kidney disease, liver disease, and so on and support fundraising for them to be able to pay for dialysis treatments among others. Many of the stations do this work for free and see this type of humanitarian work as part of their respon-sibility to their communities of operation. Ultimately, a humanitarian man-date is privileged over the commercial imperative especially when human lives are at stake. These values are in line with not just development communication values but the core values espoused in socialist television, which are grounded in equality and humanism, a development that Dr. Kwame Nkrumah would be proud of.

Toward an African Feminist Media Praxis

Throughout this book, we have seen the way that subaltern media in Ghana have addressed the needs of marginalized communities that are often excluded from mainstream media. While these media organizations begin as commercial media entities established by private individuals, they operate on the values of community and humanism that can often be in opposition to the capitalist goals that shape their operation. Although the Indigenous-language mediascape in the North is growing steadily, it is imperative to draw attention to the work of the existing media organizations that center Bilchiinsi, community and humanism at the core of their operations. It is important to pay attention to the way that these stations provide programming that not only affirms the real-ities and cultures of marginalized ethnic groups but also amplifies the voices of systematically disenfranchised groups since before Ghana's independence. Like radio in the country, these TV stations have created space for the citizenry to be more civically engaged by communicating to and with them in their first language. While some TV stations in the South are dubbing foreign content such as telenovelas in Twi, Fante, and Ga (Ussher and Ollennu, 2023), stations in the Northern Region focus efforts on developing Indigenous-language pro-gramming or amplify the regional pop culture scene by playing the music and movies of artists in the area. Some of the original content developed in Dag-banli includes personality profile programs where accomplished people from the North are invited to share their experiences to inspire the youth on pro-grams like *The Feminine Story* (Sagani TV) and *My Northern Achiever* (Zaa TV). Others are reality TV shows and competitions that are rooted in the pro-motion of the cultural values of the region. The novelty effect of television is still very much alive in this area since Indigenous-language television here is currently addressing a need in the community that has existed for decades. The anticolonial nature of the TV landscape in the Northern Region lies in its value of being a space for the community and of the community. Unlike the national film space where filmmakers are increasingly aiming to make films for an external Western gaze to gain popularity in the imperial core (Mohammed, 2025), these TV stations are responding to the geopolitical needs of their communities. This means that when they focus their work externally, they are looking to reach the Northern Ghanaian diasporic communities in other parts of Ghana, Africa, and the world. There is a growing geocultural community that consumes the broadcasts of these stations, especially through platforms like Facebook and YouTube. The simultaneous broadcasts of key programs on television and Facebook Live give new meaning to the notion of convergence.

Despite these efforts at amplifying the voices of communities in the Northern Region, some of the historical silences are reproduced since the diversity of Northern languages are not fully represented on these platforms. The primary language of transmission on Zaa TV, Sagani TV, and NTV is Dagbanli, which means that other major Northern languages such as Gonja, Kasem, Likpakpaln, and Waali are not represented on these platforms. Although stations like Zaa TV have programs like *Tamplima Saha*, which is targeted at the Tamplima community, and had planned to include programming on Mampruli, Gonja, and Bimoba in the future, these inclusions are usually tokens and often singular programs on the TV network. Other stations like NTV are already transmitting in Dagbanli and Mampruli, languages that are mutually intelligible.

We cannot talk about the important work that television is doing in Northern Ghana without examining how a key demographic like women are represented in programming and contribute on the back end to programmatic productions. Although programs such as *The Feminine Story* (Sagani TV), *ɜemana Payaba* (Zaa TV), and *The Queen Classy Show* (NTV) focus on issues affecting women, much like their Accra counterparts, they are still trapped in promoting women empowerment narratives. While the other two shows are Dagbanli shows, *The Queen Classy Show* transmits exclusively in English, which means that the majority of the women audiences who are not English speakers are excluded from it. All these shows toe the NGOization line by promoting narratives about empowerment that place the oppression of women on individual men and women rather than drawing attention to the structural roots of the issues that produce patriarchal oppression. In watching these programs over the period of seven months in 2023, I noticed that whereas *The Feminine Story* concerns itself with issues of equality and women empowerment, *ɜemana Payaba* focuses on bringing men and religious leaders as panelists to chastise women on how to be better wives among others. It was no surprise therefore that the phone-in segment of the program was dominated by men callers who mansplained to the host about how the topic under discussion should be framed and why it was important for women to be good wives, not challenge their husbands, be submissive, and so on. It is ironic that *ʒemana Paɣaba* centered the perspectives of men and reproduced patriarchal values given that the name of the program literally means "Women of this Era / Today's Woman." This draws attention to the fact that the mere existence of programming about women in media is not radical; rather, the values driving the programming, the topics discussed, and the people centered in these discussions make the programs radical. This development of antifeminist programming is not unique to stations in the North but rather is reminiscent of a larger problem in the media space of Ghana where issues affecting women such as domestic violence, sexual violence, and others are not treated with the care and nuance that they deserve (Mohammed, 2023a).

In addition, despite the liberalization of the airwaves in Ghana, manels (all-men panels convened to discuss various topics in public spaces) continue to dominate especially in programs such as the morning show, current affairs programs, and other talk shows. This development cuts across the sixteen regions of the country. While we are seeing more and more women anchoring news bulletins, we are seeing fewer women hosting "hard topic" programs such as current affairs, breakfast shows, and others. While watching the morning shows of NTV, Sagani TV, and Zaa TV in most of 2023, I found that very few women appeared as panelists on these programs where partisan politics were discussed. During these programs when women were occasionally platformed, they were sometimes subjected to sexist attacks by their fellow panelists and audience members who phoned into the program. Toward the end of 2023, there were virtually no women appearing as guests on these morning shows, a development that can be attributed to the misogyny they were often subjected to. Therefore, although Indigenous-language TV stations are disrupting the status quo by amplifying the silenced histories and realities of marginalized ethnic groups, on the flip side they can reinforce the status quo by platforming and reinscribing harmful narratives about gender.

As we saw in earlier chapters, religion plays a crucial role in shaping the political economy of media in Ghana. In the case of filmmaking, film production in the Northern Region is structured in such a way that little to no production is done during the Ramadan/Nolori period. Similarly, during this period, certain major programs on TV are suspended in order to cede the airwaves to Muslim clerics to come on the air to preach to the masses. Some of the clerics use these programs to chastise women about how they dress, how they relate to their husbands, and how they carry themselves in public. While we are seeing a gradual global uptick in interest around Islamic feminisms and bringing a more feminist approach to Islam by demonstrating how the religion can work to create space for marginalized people such as women, LGBTQI+ people, disabled people, and others to live dignified lives in the Ummah, the opposite can be said to be true not just in the Muslim religious space of the Northern Region but in the Christian religious space in the South and at the national level. Therefore, we can make a direct connection between the proliferation of religious content and the erasure of women not just in the public space but also in certain types of programming on media platforms. For example, in one of my conversations with my interlocutors, they received tremendous pushback from Islamic clerics in Tamale for promoting Dagbaŋ culture through the *Simpa Dance Competition* reality TV program where women asserted bodily autonomy in these dances. These clerics found it offensive that women participated in these programs and sought to find ways to put an end to this program that has not just become an instant hit with the masses but also promoted the revival of aspects of Dagbaŋ culture that were at threat of extinction.

Beyond the disdain that Muslim clerics have for programs where women assert their bodily autonomy, some of the clerics have sought to erase the celebrations of other cultural festivals such as Buɣum that have been an integral part of the cultural landscape for centuries. This treatment of African cultures and knowledges through an Arab supremacist lens in the name of Islamic religion is no different from the process of deculturation and de-linguicization that Christian missionaries subjected and are still subjecting African communities to. This erasure does not just stop at the marginalization of women but also pushes hard for the erasure of African cultures. Therefore, as we commend these media organizations for doing important cultural work to preserve, promote, and affirm African cultures, languages, philosophies, and knowledges, it is important to hold them accountable for creating space for the reproduction of colonial logics through Eastern influences such as Islam. What then becomes the role of decolonial television? How can decolonial television uphold African cultures that are threatened by Eastern and Western imperialism while imagining liberatory futures for all community members? What role can African feminisms rooted in Indigenous knowledges play in safeguarding African cultures and the dignity of marginalized African people? How can we pull from Bilchiinsi and other African philosophies to ensure that we preserve the radical and decolonial aspects of the cultures of our ancestors while resisting oppression and imperialism from the East and the West?

Conclusion

• •

Resisting Cultural Imperialism

Ʒiri yirigi pum, ka yɛlimaŋli diee wali

Throughout this book, we have seen the connections between colonization, culture, and media. I take a step beyond drawing these connections by demonstrating the way that alternative media at the margins are leading the charge in the efforts at decolonizing media and culture through Indigenous knowledges, languages, and philosophies. Through amplifying the narratives and knowledge-making cultures of communities that have historically been disenfranchised by colonization, the current iteration of the nation-state, and this wave of new media affordances, we learn about the globality of colonial imperialism and the parallels between Indigenous knowledges in Africa, the Americas, and Oceania, among others.

These connections of oppressions between Global South communities both inside and outside the imperial core demonstrate the importance of building solidarities while emphasizing the mutuality that solidarity building should be based on. Indigenous communities in the United States and Canada have so much to learn from Indigenous communities in Global Majority countries and vice versa, especially with regard to knowledge building and antiracist, anticapitalist, and anticolonialist organizing. By understanding the importance of culture making in media spaces, we bring attention to the need for building solidarities on the common ground of the interlocked oppressions that these communities are subjected to. While there is currently a wave to decolonize everything, our understanding of decolonization cannot be divorced from the roots of this project, which is based in the historical colonization and current neocolonialism of Global South communities. This means that decolonization is an epistemological, ontological, and axiological project that is intertwined with the land back movement, the movement for reparations for Africa and its diaspora for the enslavement of Africans, the return of sacred and culturally symbolic artifacts to colonized communities, the dismantling of imperialism in the economic, cultural, and political senses, and the promotion of the rights of all marginalized communities utilizing the praxis of Bilchiinsi and ubuntu philosophies.

Throughout the book, I not only demonstrated in practical ways how media at the margins have charted a pathway in the process of decolonization but also interrogated the fundamental taken-for-grantedness embedded in the knowledge production process, which is rooted in eurocentric values and can lead to the reproduction of coloniality especially when cocreating knowledge with marginalized communities. I ask here that we reimagine why we cocreate knowledge, with whom we cocreate knowledge, for whom we cocreate knowledge, and what legacies we hope to build with the knowledge we produce. This means pulling from the roots the supposed conventions around knowledge production that are grounded in white supremacist, capitalist, patriarchal values and looking to Indigenous communities that have historically produced knowledge grounded in an ethic of care, communality, collectivism, and human dignity.

I ask that we turn globalization on its head and examine it through a lens of power while paying attention to who has the tools and resources to be able to globalize their nation-state in the cultural, political, and economic senses. I am referring to what countries are positioned to gain global attention and recognition with their cultural products (Mohammed, 2025). Here too we need to leverage the technological tools available to us—technologies that are built on the exploitation of Indigenous communities in the Global South— to develop strong global networks of solidarity that center the material reality of Indigenous communities peripheralized by the imperial core. As we interrogate power in this way, we need to be cognizant of the importance of understanding the historical precedent for which countries wield power and which countries don't and how the Global Minority (Western countries) wield and deploy this power in ways that have led to the economic exploitation of Global Majority countries (formerly colonized nations) and the way this desire for economic power necessitates that these powerful countries wage wars and perpetrate genocides against people in places like Palestine, Afghanistan, Somalia, the Democratic Republic of Congo, Sudan, and others.

Globalization has brought with it attendant issues such as cultural imperialism, which can be more easily deployed using digital platforms such as social media and streaming technologies. According to Moyo (2020, p. 12), "In most African countries, modern forms of cultural imperialism are inextricable from the local content philosophies and practices of local media." Although digital platforms have the potential to support organizing work for radical praxis, they have been appropriated in support of colonialist and imperialist propaganda through the news, pop culture, music, and other modes of entertainment media. According to Samir Amin, at its very core colonization was one of the earliest forms of globalization (Tricontinental: Institute for Social Research, 2018). Therefore, globalization cannot be delinked from the enslavement of African peoples for the benefit of the Global North. This is why we need to be cautious of our uncritical celebration of globalization, which is grounded in the extraction of African cultural products, mineral resources, and raw materials for the benefit of the imperial core. We saw in this book how intranational and transnational politics shape not just the political economy of media but the ideologies that drive media production and representations. I reiterate here the importance of Africanizing media systems and making them relevant to the lived reality of Africans. This would mean moving away from performing for an external imperialist gaze and toward preserving African languages and cultures and supporting their growth (Mohammed, 2025).

Media, especially entertainment media, are used by world powers like the United States to manufacture consent in the global public sphere to justify these atrocities that not only take thousands of human lives but have devastating impacts for the environment and its inhabitants, atrocities that generations of these targeted communities have paid for and continue to pay for. Not only is this globality of the manufacture of consent by imperialist nations important to pay attention to, it demonstrates how cultural imperialism can be deployed to set the agenda for what topics the world should be concerned about. The military-entertainment-industrial complex (militainment) in Hollywood, which is largely controlled by the U.S. Department of Defense, has done a tremendous job of funding and supporting the normalization of U.S. war and imperialist propaganda (Stahl, 2010). As we think of the proliferation of Hollywood militainment movies around the world, we need to examine how they manufacture consent both at home and abroad and what this means for the normalization of nation-state-sanctioned violence via militarism in the pursuit of wealth.

Hollywood militainment movies such as *Top Gun* have promoted U.S. military and imperialist propaganda at home and abroad. Others like *American Sniper* glorify America's military-industrial complex by using moving images to rewrite war narratives and normalize U.S. imperialist violence in the Middle East while constructing these communities as deserving of this violence. What then does this proliferation of war propaganda media from the most powerful country in the world mean for the nascent culture industries of Global South countries who often don't have state backing in the production of movies? How can we understand the growth of Global South culture industries that have the potential to project the anticolonial values of communities at the margins of both the imperial core and the postcolonial nation-state? What are the implications of this type of cultural imperialism on the knowledge structures, languages, and ways of life of the Global South?

The Future of Subaltern Media

In contending with the process of decolonization, there is the need to understand the complexities around colonization and the reproduction of hegemonies both within the nation-state and in transnational and global spaces. Whereas the widely accepted understanding of postcolonialism points to the relationship between newly created nation-states—through imperialist expansion in the partition of Africa—and their former colonizers, I have shown in this book that postcolonialism presents us with the tools to understand the current neocolonial reality of many Global South countries. Here, we see that the boundaries between the old and the new even in colonial processes are blurred as colonization finds new spaces to thrive in the neocolonial relationships to which the Global South is held hostage. By drawing parallels between global/transnational hegemonies and intranational hegemonies, we begin to deconstruct the complexities of colonization and how the elevation of certain ethnic and cultural groups within the nation-state by the bourgeois elite class can reproduce the colonization of more marginalized ethnic groups and languages. The media therefore becomes a space where power is reasserted by groups dominant based on class and ethnicity to control representations of language, culture, and identity. Revisiting Nkrumah's goals of using media for social transformation by making it accessible to the masses is a good place to start. In addition, mainstream media can learn from Indigenous-language media how to create the conditions for the masses to claim ownership of these culture-making and culture-affirming spaces.

As we have seen throughout the book, colonization can manifest as silencing, erasure, and de-agentization and sometimes outrightly misrepresenting communities that are subjected to intranational and international cultural imperialism. As we grapple with linguicide and linguifam as a fundamental part of the process of deculturalization, attention needs to be paid to the way that these processes replicate colonial values of hierarchies and hegemonies produced among communities within the same nation-state. Although some of these values around the reproduction of hegemonies may have already existed before the enslavement of Africans and the creation of nation-states, colonization played an integral role in amplifying these hierarchies by creating the mediator class in order to better enslave and colonize these communities. This mediator class has evolved to become the comprador class or the elite class that serves as caretakers of the postcolonial nation on behalf of Western powers. They are not just mere caretakers but have worked their way to becoming the oppressor class that participates in capturing the nation-state for their selfish economic interests and the imperialist interests of colonizers. This class also does the work of maintaining what Young (2016) calls "bourgeois nationalism." In this sense, bourgeois nationalism centers the interests of the comprador class while promoting dominant cultures through national symbols and their myopic notions around constructing a unified national identity: a process that further erases, silences, and de-agentizes marginalized ethnicities, languages, and cultures.

This "internal cultural imperialism" (Salih, 2021) demonstrates the double bind that marginalized ethnic groups in the nation-state are subjected to. This phenomenon is not unique to Ghana but can be observed in various countries in Africa and beyond where dominant ethnic groups that often produce the nation's elite class determine what national identity looks like and what languages represent the nation's essence. For example, in Ghana, Akan is the dominant identity that shapes national symbols and national cultural mythologies. In countries like Nigeria, we hear of the Hausa, Yoruba, and Igbo people, while the many other ethnicities are symbolically erased in the national imaginary. Similarly, in Senegal, we learn about the Wolof people and how their cultural identity shapes the national imaginary. It is therefore unsurprising that these dominant groups' cultural products are the ones that make it to the global space. This internal cultural colonization means that while dominant groups like the Akan fight to export their culture in the face of continental and global erasure by dominant African countries like Nigeria, marginalized ethnic groups in Ghana have to grapple with a double marginalization where they simultaneously fight for national and global visibility. For these doubly marginalized communities, global visibility feels like a pipe dream that is merely aspirational.

In this book, I have deconstructed colonization and decolonization using a specific community in Ghana that has been subjected to political, economic, educational, and cultural marginalization within this postcolonial nation-state. By situating this conversation within continental and global discussions of decolonization, I demonstrate that the process of decolonization needs to expand the notion of activism to understand the potential that media has to not only complement organizing but be a space of radical decolonial praxis. In each chapter, I make connections between media and the historical reality of Ghana and why it is important to ground media praxis in Indigenous knowledge systems and the praxis of decolonization. By putting Northern Ghanaian media in conversation with national, continental, and global media politics, I demonstrate the globality of colonization and the importance of espousing a global approach to conceptualizing, interrogating, and dismantling colonial and imperialist structures that are intricately woven into global capitalism. I ultimately draw connections between media evolution and development, to build a coherent argument about why the current media realities of Ghana and many other postcolonial communities are the way that they are. The media economies of these countries can be marginalized intranationally, transnationally, and globally depending on the power dynamics at play and how they intertwine with historical, cultural, and economic factors to produce marginality. Therefore, my discussion of transnational subalternity and the work of lunsi/griots to preserve, sustain, and transmit knowledge, cultures, philosophies, and traditions challenges us to rethink dominant ideologies around knowledge and the validity of knowledge.

In decolonizing media in Africa and other parts of the Global South, it is imperative for us to reconceptualize what constitutes media in the pedagogical and epistemological senses. This would mean departing from Manichean conceptualizations that classify media into categories such as old and new, traditional and contemporary, among many others. The political economy of media in Africa teaches us that the old and new, the traditional and contemporary blur into each other, feed each other, and complement each other to sustain media ecologies or create media phenomena that are reflective of and useful for the time and space in which they are born. Radio, television, film, and social and digital media are speaking to each other and informing one another in ways that early media creators, inventors, and scholars may not have imagined. For example, podcasting has taken radio and reimagined it in the digital space, tacking on various affordances for this crop of audiences. Streaming by way of Netflix, Hulu, and Amazon Prime Video has radically reconceptualized television in the areas of production, distribution, and consumption. Across various African countries, mobile phone technologies have radically transformed banking and business transactions by way of M-Pesa and Momo (mobile money) to make it accessible to populations who otherwise would be excluded from these "formal" processes. However, the way that "new" media builds on "old" media is not a novel concept; the only novel feature of it is how these media interactions speak to the future of media convergence and how this may complicate the way that media is produced in the future.

We cannot discuss the future of media in Africa and the globe without discussing the globalization of streaming platforms. I contend that we need to be mindful of how we tend to uncritically celebrate the globalization of entertainment media platforms such as Netflix. A development like this only lines the pockets of a handful of filmmakers and creatives in select Global South and European countries while further marginalizing filmmakers and communities that do not have the social capital to work their way into lucrative Netflix deals. In Africa, Netflix is making inroads into Nigeria and South Africa (two of some of the most economically powerful African nations) while further marginalizing the culture industries of othered African countries such as Burkina Faso, Mali, Equatorial Guinea, Sudan, Cabo Verde, and Malawi, among others. Here, the legacies of colonization dictate whose culture is selected to be exploited for the consumption of the cosmopolitan global audience community.

An iteration of Anglo-American dominance colors these celebrations of African stories given that African countries colonized by France, Portugal, and Spain are erased from these celebrations because they are not part of the global Anglo minority community. In this decolonization process, language has always been an important site of contestation given the duty that language has to hold the cultures, traditions, and values of a people. In this neocolonial reality, language has always been a site of struggle, which means that marginalized languages are erased in favor of dominant often colonial languages, a development that results in linguifam (wa Thiong'o, 2009) and linguicide. Ultimately, there is a reproduction of language hegemony in which stories get told on national media and streaming platforms, a situation that isn't that different from the struggle that the Indigenous-language media landscape in many African countries grapples with. These politics of representation that replicate hegemonies parallel the politics of representation in imperial core nations such as the United States, where the realities of Indigenous communities are silenced and erased and when represented are filtered through a colonial lens that plays on tropes that amplify the supposed barbarity and savagery of these communities. Here too the experiences of Indigenous nations with smaller populations tend to get subsumed in the stories of the more widely known communities. The struggle therefore is to be truly inclusive rather than just creating media that amplify the stories of major ethnic groups and languages with the largest populations.

There is another layer to this erasure where the stories of marginalized ethnic groups in South Africa and Nigeria (much like in Ghana) do not get to enjoy these so-called dividends of the globalization of Netflix. South Africa has made some inroads to tackle the cultural imperialism that may come with the influx of Netflix in the country's streaming space. By imposing a 30 percent local content quota on streaming platforms (Motsaathebe and Chiumbu, 2021), South Africa is not just safeguarding its culture industries but creating the conditions for the jobs and revenue that may come with local productions staying within the country. This development is not that different from media quota policies in the European Union that aim to safeguard local/continental languages, media economies, and cultures. While this may not seem like a sustainable solution to the threat of cultural imperialism that the Global South is subjected to, it is a place to start. Many African countries can learn from the South Africa example to ensure that their culture industries are not subsumed in this supposed wave of globalization by streaming.

Toward a Radical Media Praxis

In resisting imperialism intra- and internationally, publicly funded media may need to be reimagined to more directly challenge colonization and the reproduction of hierarchies. Even though GBC worked to grow their impact across the various regions by establishing local GBC radio stations, not much has been done on the television front to create space for the promotion, representation, and celebration of marginalized Ghanaian languages. Instead of issuing licenses to religious leaders and businesspeople to promote foods and drugs that have not been approved by the Food and Drugs Authority (FDA), media regulatory bodies can work toward strengthening the civic space by limiting the issuance of licenses to these actors. Rather, the resources should be channeled toward building a more robust civic space where as many Ghanaian languages as possible are represented, especially in regional media. GBC can also build affiliate relationships with already existing commercial television stations to build their capacity to provide more diverse linguistic representation in their regions of operation.

In addition, a shift from fulfilling the commercial imperative may be a productive place to start to begin working toward promoting the media and culture industries of marginalized communities that may be faced with the double bind of the harmful effects of globalization and the cultural hegemonies replicated in the nation-states that they are located in. This is one of many steps toward tackling linguicide head-on while promoting the growth of culture industries that are affirming of marginalized communities.

In an anti-imperialist media dispensation, the gender, cultural, and geographical diversity of this imposed identity of nationalism is not only celebrated but portrayed with the nuances and complexities that define them. In this future, media organizations work toward dismantling the reproduction of historical silences that have been amplified and entrenched by (neo)colonial domination and control. One of the major struggles that commercial media organizations in Ghana face today is the challenge to stay in business while more and more media organizations are granted licenses to operate in a very small market. This challenge to be financially viable may in the long run challenge the work that Indigenous-language media in the country (especially the North) are doing to maintain the cultural and linguistic sovereignty of the communities they serve. Nevertheless, the cultural ownership that marginalized ethnic groups have over commercial Indigenous-language media organizations such as radio and television is radical in the way that it impacts these communities' abilities to resist internal colonization by other dominant groups while serving their core audiences in the community and the national and global diasporas of these ethnic groups.

Beyond resisting internal and external imperialism, Indigenous-language media organizations still have a long way to go as far as representing the complexities of marginalization in Ghana is concerned. As Ghana becomes increasingly religious, there is the risk that media programming will eventually be overrun by religious dogma (both Christian and Muslim) to (re)shape popular and cultural notions about gender, sexuality, and disability, among others.

Many Indigenous-language stations in Northern and Southern Ghana are already beholden to the money that mosques and churches bring to buy airtime to preach the gospel. While this inundation of religious content on Indigenous-language media in the North is reduced to Fridays and the Ramadan period, it is much more extensive in the South, where preachers establish entire TV stations to preach the gospel around the clock. The North is well on its way to this reality as the clergy gains more power in the national public sphere. For example, in the Northern Region, the proliferation of Islamic religious programming on television and radio is shaping the everyday experiences of women due to the way that this male-dominated space tends to promote sexist ideas about women and womanhood while drowning out cultural values and conventions that created the conditions for women to take up space in public. Imperialism here looks like the imposition of Muslim and Arab cultures on this community, leading to the gradual erasure of Northern cultures especially in metropolitan areas.

A decolonial future grapples with the impact of Western and Eastern cultures in Africa that support the erasure and symbolic annihilation of African cultures, languages, and philosophies. A decolonial media future is grounded in communality, collectivism, and Bilchiinsi philosophies. It centers marginalized communities and works toward challenging imperialism while reflecting on and rethinking ways to promote the radical aspects of African cultures while discarding the aspects of the culture that are oppressive toward disenfranchised communities. A decolonial media future is grounded in the mutuality of global solidarity while drawing attention to the globality and everydayness of colonization. It is rooted in the essence of Bilchiinsi and ubuntu philosophies.

Acknowledgments

This book is a product of years of work grounded in community knowledge and supported by my immediate and extended family. I am grateful to nba Mohammed and nma Salamatu for their patience and openness in answering all my questions about Dagbaŋ cultures, traditions, and epistemologies. Thanks to nba for raising me to be brave and fearless and stand for truth and justice no matter what. My brothers, Mandieya and Tiyumtaba, have been unwavering in their support of me and my quest to document our knowledge systems. Alina Aftab has been a wonderful ear and shoulder to lean on throughout the years. Shakia Asamoah read this book in its very early drafts as a dissertation and generously provided editorial support.

For my baby, Paɣasana, what a delightful soul.

This project began as a dissertation for my PhD in mass communications at The Pennsylvania State University. It has since evolved beyond my wildest dreams. I am thankful to Dr. Anthony Olorunnisola for being an integral part of my academic career and for being available to answer my endless questions about the academy. Dr. Gabeba Baderoon's thoughtfulness, kindness, and commitment to justice are qualities I can only aspire to. I am grateful to have learned from and been in community with Dr. Maha Maroun and Dr. Michelle Rodino-Colocino. Their insights on feminisms and media not only have shaped this book but have also made me a better scholar. Dr. Kevin Hagopian's contribution to shaping the initial stages of this project and availability to talk about everything pedagogy have made me a better scholar and teacher. Research assistant extraordinaire Lukman Mahami Adams's hard work kept me on task and supported the completion of my dissertation project on time.

I cannot talk about how this book came to be without acknowledging nbieli, Alhassan Yushawu Jahanfo, who has been one of my main sources of inspiration to pursue and cocreate knowledge on Indigenous-language media.

Working side by side with him as a teenager in the newsroom of Fiila FM intrigued me and set me on the path of connecting Indigenous knowledges to contemporary media. He continues to be my number one cheerleader and I am so grateful for his wisdom and bilchiinsi.

Professor Amin Alhassan not only has been a mentor but has paved the way for us to imagine new worlds in beautifully liberatory ways. Thanks to Dr. Eliasu Mumuni and the University for Development Studies, Tamale for their endless support of me and my work. I am grateful to Kwame Acheampong of Abdul Hameed Pictures for working with me to beautifully capture the essence of the media community in Tamale for this book. My collaborator and older brother Mohammed Sheriff Yamusah (Sheriff Ghale), whose scholarship has inspired me in so many ways, is a guiding light in my quest to cocreate knowledge with my community. He also provided translations for the proverb epigraphs. Thank you.

I am thankful to my village of mentors who held, nurtured, and guided me on this project and many others. This book is stronger because Dr. Sylvia Bawa, Dr. Ismael Montana, Dr. Girish Daswani, Dr. Msia Kibona Clark, Dr. Anandam Kavoori, Dr. Kemi Balogun took the time to read chapters of the book and provide generous feedback. Dr. Sylvia Bawa's moral and intellectual support has kept me strong in times of adversity. Dr. Jarpa Dawuni's commitment to justice has paved the way for people like me to know that because she could, I can too. I am grateful to Dr. Kemi Balogun for providing initial guidance on this project, for her sisterhood, and for her patience in answering all my ridiculous questions. Dr. Anandam Kavoori is the mentor I never expected to have but who always showed up to support me whenever I needed him to. I am thankful to Dr. Aswin Punathambekar for his mentorship and for helping me to navigate the editorial process for this project. I am grateful to Dr. Maryann Erigha for showing up whenever I needed her to. I am so very lucky to have an older sister in Dr. Msia Kibona Clark who respects and values me and is always available to listen to me vent about my frustrations about academic culture. Asante!

I am thankful to my editor Nicole Solano for seeking me out, for believing in this book, and for affirming my voice. Thanks to everyone at Rutgers University Press who have supported in myriad ways to make this book a reality.

This project would not have been possible without support from the Bellisario College of Communications and a grant from the Don Davis Program in Ethical Leadership at the Pennsylvania State University. I am grateful to the Office of the Provost at the University of Georgia for supporting this project with grant funding. Funding from the Sarah Moss Fellowship at the University of Georgia, which enabled me to spend my research leave in Ghana in 2023, was instrumental to the completion of this book. Thanks to the Department of Communication at Cornell University which provided a home for me to do the finishing touches on the book.

Several chapters of this book were written in the greenhouse at the State Botanical Garden of Georgia in Athens, my happy place! I am grateful to all the workers and groundskeepers for working endlessly to maintain the serenity, calm, and sublimity of this space.

Thanks to everyone who in one way or the other supported this project to fruition.

The following chapters are derived in part from previously published articles:

Introduction: Mohammed, W. F. (2021). Decolonizing African media studies. *Howard Journal of Communications*, *32*(2), 123–138. https://doi.org/10.1080/10646175.2021.1871868. Copyright © Taylor & Francis Group, LLC.

Chapter 1: Mohammed, W. F. (2022). Bilchiinsi philosophy: Decolonizing methodologies in media studies. *Review of Communication*, *22*(1), 7–24. https://doi.org/10.1080/15358593.2021.2024870. Copyright © National Communication Association, 1765 N Street NW, Washington, DC 20036.

Chapter 4: Mohammed, W. F. (2022). Globalisation and Indigenous cinemas: A history of Ghanaian Dagbanli films. *Journal of International Communication*, *28*(2), 286–305. https://doi.org/10.1080/13216597.2022.2073256. Copyright © Macquarie University, Sydney, NSW 2109, Australia.

The Chapter Proverbs
and Their Translations

The Dagbanli proverbs found at the top of each chapter were translated by
Mohammed Sheriff Yamusah (Sheriff Ghale), a faculty member in the department of Theatre and Performing Arts at the University for Development Studies.

Introduction: Decolonizing African Media Studies
Sɔli din viɛla ni laɣim so'chandiba
A good route gathers many travelers

Chapter 1: Bilchiinsi Philosophy, Media, and Global Indigenous Epistemologies
Bia ŋun nu viɛla ŋuni n samdi kpiɛm dɔri
A child whose hands are clean serves the elder's meal

Chapter 2: Technology, Literacy, and Media Development in Northern Ghana
Biɛla biɛla ndaa nam wɔbgu
Little drops of water make the mighty ocean

Chapter 3: Subalterns, Griots, and Media
A yi bɔli a yuli n ti lunsi nyin di lahi sɔyiri zama ni
You cannot hide at the gathering, after announcing your title to the drummers

Chapter 4: African Cinemas, Globalization, and Resistance
O di mali mali
Baya bila di mali mali ti paai tuɔm
He enjoyed sweets
The young soothsayer enjoyed sweets until he tasted bitterness

Chapter 5: Movie Distribution, Urban Architecture, and the Newsification of Movies
Kookali lana n wumdi jɛbɔbgi kumsi
Only the wise hear when a hair louse cries

Chapter 6: Television for Social Change
Sagani ku tooi kari saa, naɣila saa n pun je mibu
The rainbow drives away only clouds that did not mean to rain

Conclusion: Resisting Cultural Imperialism
Ʒiri yirigi pum, ka yɛlimaŋli diee wali
A lie only blooms, for the truth to bear fruits

References

Adamu, A. U. (2007). Currying favour: Eastern media influences and the Hausa video film. *Film International*, *5*(4), 77–89. https://doi.org/10.1386/fiin.5.4.77

——. (2010). The muse's journey: Transcultural translators and the domestication of Hindi music in Hausa popular culture. *Journal of African Cultural Studies*, *22*(1), 41–56. https://doi.org/10.1080/13696810903488579

Aggoh, R. A., and Siabi-Mensah, K. (2003). *Literacy: A key to development. The GILLBT literacy programme in Ghana.* Ghana Universities Press.

Albuquerque, A. d. (2021). The institutional basis of anglophone Western centrality. *Media, Culture & Society*, *43*(1), 180–188. https://doi.org/10.1177/0163443720957893

Alhassan, A. (2005). Market valorization in broadcasting policy in Ghana: Abandoning the quest for media democratization. *Media, Culture & Society*, *27*(2), 211–228.

Al-hassan, S., Andani, A., and Abdul-Malik, A. (2011). The role of community radio in livelihood improvement: The case of Simli Radio. *Field Actions Science Reports*, *5*, 1–6.

Amoakohene, M. I. (2004). Researching radio audiences in an emerging pluralistic media environment: A case for the focus group discussion (FGD) method. *Africa Media Review 12*(2), 25–40.

Amoh, E. (2022). Revisiting Kwame Nkrumah's African personality: The diaspora context and the making of Ghana television. *Ghana Studies*, *25*, 33–56.

Andani, M. I., and Antwi-Boateng, O. (2021). FM stations' role in rural development: The case of Northern Ghana. *Perspectives on Global Development & Technology*, *20*(4), 336–357. https://doi.org/10.1163/15691497-12341599

Ansah, P. A. V. (1986). Broadcasting and multilingualism. In G. Wedell, J. Kangwana and L. Lawler (Eds.), *Making broadcasting useful: The African experience* (pp. 47–65). Manchester University Press.

Asante, G. A. (2019). #RhetoricSoWhite and US centered: Reflections on challenges and opportunities. *Quarterly Journal of Speech*, *105*(4), 484–488. https://doi.org/10.1080/00335630.2019.1669892

Ashcroft, B., Griffiths, G., & Tiffin, H. (2000). *Post-colonial studies: the key concepts.* Routledge.

Aveh, A. (2010). The rise of the video film industry and its projected social impact on Ghanaians. *African Literature Today, 28*, 122–132.

———. (2014). The "Nigerianization" of Ghanaian eyes. *Journal of African Cinemas, 6*, 109–122.

Banjo, O. O. (Ed.). (2019). *Media across the African diaspora: Content, audiences, and global influence.* Routledge.

Barlet, O. (2010). Bollywood/Africa: A divorce? *Black Camera, 2*(1), 126–143. https://doi.org/10.2979/BLC.2010.2.1.126

Barnard, I. (2006). The language of multiculturalism in South African soaps and sitcoms. *Journal of Multicultural Discourses, 1*(1), 39–59. https://doi.org/10.1080/10382040608668531

Blankson, I. A. (2005). Negotiating the use of native languages in emerging pluralistic and independent broadcast systems in Africa. *African Media Review, 13*(1), 1–22.

Blaylock, J. (2022). The mother, the mistress, and the cover girls: Ghana broadcasting corporation and the coloniality of gender. *Feminist Media Histories, 8*(1), 102–133.

Césaire, A., Kelley, R. D. G., and Pinkham, J. (2000). *Discourse on colonialism.* Monthly Review Press.

Chakravartty, P., Kuo, R., Grubbs, V., and McIlwain, C. (2018). #Communication-SoWhite. *Journal of Communication, 68*(2), 254–266. https://doi.org/10.1093/joc/jqy003

Chernoff, J. M. (1979). *African rhythm and African sensibility: Aesthetics and social action in African musical idioms.* University of Chicago Press.

Chigudu, S. (2019). *Blindspots; Or is it ethical for white people to study Africa?* [Paper]. European Conference on African Studies, Edinburgh, Scotland.

Chilisa, B., Major, T. E., and Khudu-Petersen, K. (2017). Community engagement with a postcolonial, African-based relational paradigm. *Qualitative Research, 17*(3), 326–339. https://doi.org/10.1177/1468794117696176

Clark, M. K. & Mohammed, W. F. (2023). *African women in digital spaces: Redefining social movements on the continent and in the diaspora.* Mkuki na Nyota.

Collins, P. H. (2009). *Black feminist thought: Knowledge, consciousness, and the politics of empowerment.* Routledge.

Crenshaw, K. (1991). Mapping the margins: Intersectionality, identity politics, and violence against women of color. *Stanford Law Review, 43*(6), 1241–1299

Cruz, J. M. (2015). Reimagining feminist organizing in global times: Lessons from African feminist communication. *Women & Language, 38*(1), 23–41.

Dabiri, E. (2014, January 21). Why I'm not an Afropolitan. *Africa Is a Country.* https://africasacountry.com/2014/01/why-im-not-an-afropolitan/

Dagbamba. (past and present). "Bilchiinsi." *Dagbaŋ Philosophy.* Northern Ghana.

Daugherty, M. (2022, September 18). Radio's dead, but we're still dancing. *Bowdoin Review.* https://bowdoinreview.com/2022/09/18/radios-dead-but-were-still-dancing/

Dennis, A. (2018). Promoting Ghana's traditional cultural aesthetics in Ghana's Most Beautiful reality television show. *Legon Journal of the Humanities, 29*(2), 176–196. https://doi.org/10.4314/ljh.v29i2.7

Dutta, M. J., & Pal, M. (2020). Theorizing from the Global South: Dismantling, resisting, and transforming communication theory. *Communication Theory, 30*(4), 349–369. https://doi.org/10.1093/ct/qtaa010

Fisher, A. (2016). Modes of griot inscription in African cinema. *Journal of African Media Studies, 8*(1), 5–16. https://doi.org/10.1386/jams.8.1.5_1

————. (2018). African cinema on demand? The politics of online distribution and the case of the African film library. *Journal of African Media Studies, 10*(3), 239–250. https://doi.org/10.1386/jams.10.3.239_1

Fosu, M. (2011). Situating language at the centre of journalism training: The case for broadening the spheres of English teaching and learning in journalism training institutions in Ghana. *Global Media Journal—African Edition, 5*(1), 52–80. https://doi.org/10.5789/5-1-57

Gadzekpo, A. (2009). Missing links: African media studies and feminist concerns. *Journal of African Media Studies, 1*(1), 69–80. https://doi.org/10.1386/jams.1.1.69_1

Garritano, C. (2013). *African video movies and global desires: A Ghanaian history.* Ohio University Press.

Ghana Broadcasting Corporation. (n.d.). About Us. https://www.gbcvoice.com/about/

Ghana Statistical Service. (2022a). *Ghana 2021 Population and Housing Census* (Vol. 3). *General Report.* Retrieved February 27, 2024, from https://census2021.statsghana .gov.gh/gssmain/fileUpload/reportthemelist/Volume%203%20Highlights.pdf

————. (2022b, September). *Illiteracy in Ghana: Trends, Patterns and Correlates. Thematic Brief.* Retrieved February 27, 2024, from https://census2021.statsghana .gov.gh/gssmain/fileUpload/reportthemesub/Illiteracy%20in%20Ghana%20-%20 Trends%20Patterns%20and%20Correlates.pdf

Ghanaweb. (2017). Kumkum Bhagya stars arrive in Ghana. Retrieved July 15, 2019, from https://www.ghanaweb.com/GhanaHomePage/entertainment/Kumkum -Bhagya-stars-arrive-in-Ghana-601544

Glück, A. (2018). De-Westernization and decolonization in media studies. In M. Powers (Ed.), *Oxford research encyclopedia of communication.* Oxford University Press. https://doi.org/10.1093/acrefore/9780190228613.013.898

Gourlay, K. A. (2001). Goge. *Grove Music Online.* https://doi.org/10.1093/gmo /9781561592630.article.11365

Hale, T. A. (2007). *Griots and griottes: Masters of words and music.* Indiana University Press.

Hamid, M. (2010). *The influence of Islam on an African people: The case of the Dagomba of Northern Ghana* [Paper]. International Conference on Universalism, Relativism & Intercultural Philosophy.

Huxtable, S. (2018). What was socialist television and what came next? *European Journal of Communication, 33*(1), 89–96. https://doi.org/10.1177/0267323117753739

IDE-JETRO. (n.d.). *Electricity company of Ghana.* Retrieved November 7, 2023, from https://www.ide.go.jp/English/Data/Africa_file/Company/ghana02.html

Ihejirika, W. C. (2009). Muslim minorities and media access in a predominantly Christian city: The case of Port Harcourt, Nigeria. *Journal of African Media Studies, 1*(3), 469–491. https://doi:10.1386/jams.1.3.469/1

India TV News. (2017, October 18). West Africa's crazy love for "Kumkum Bhagya"; Ghana U-17 team wants to meet Abhi and Pragya in real life. Retrieved July 15, 2019, from https://www.indiatvnews.com/entertainment/tv-kumkum-bhagya -ekta-kapoor-tv-show-popular-in-ghana-u-17-football-team-looking-forward-to -meet-abhi-pragya-in-real-life-407273

Information Services Department. (2020). About ISD. https://isd.gov.gh/

International Trade Administration. (2022, July 22). *Ghana—Country commercial guide: Energy and renewables.* Retrieved September 11, 2023, from https://www .trade.gov/country-commercial-guides/ghana-energy-and-renewables

Isika, G. U., and Assay, B. E. (2008). Factoring local media into peace building process: A Niger Delta perspective. In E. M. Mojaye, E. Arhagba, E. Soola, and L. Oso (Eds.), *Media, dialogue, peace building and reconciliation*. Book Wright Nigeria.

Jeater, D. (2018). Academic standards or academic imperialism? Zimbabwean perceptions of hegemonic power in the global construction of knowledge. *African Studies Review, 61*(2), 8–27.

Kaschula, R. H. (1999). Imbongi and griot: Toward a comparative analysis of oral poetics in southern and west Africa. *Journal of African Cultural Studies, 12*(1), 55–76.

Kraidy, M. M. (2002). Hybridity in cultural globalization. *Communication Theory, 12*(3), 316–339. https://doi.org/10.1111/j.1468-2885.2002.tb00272.x

Larkin, B. (2008). *Signal and noise: Media, infrastructure, and urban culture in Nigeria*. Duke University Press.

Lobato, R. (2019). *Netflix nations: The geography of digital distribution*. New York University Press.

Loomba, A. (2005). *Colonialism/Postcolonialism* (2nd ed.). Routledge.

MacGaffey, W. (2013). *Chiefs, priests, and praise-singers: History, politics, and land ownership in Northern Ghana*. University of Virginia Press.

Mahama, I. (2009). *A colonial history of Northern Ghana*. GILLBT.

Makana, S. (2018). Contested encounters: Toward a twenty-first-century African feminist ethnography. *Meridians, 17*(2), 361–375. https://doi.org/10.1215/15366936-7176516

May, V. M. (2015). *Pursuing intersectionality, unsettling dominant imaginaries*. Routledge.

Mboti, N., and Tomaselli, K. (2015). New political economies of film distribution for South Africa's townships? A critical survey of the ReaGilè concept. *Critical Arts, 29*(5), 621–643. https://doi.org/10.1080/02560046.2015.1125093

Melkote, S. R., and Steeves, H. L. (2015). *Communication for development: Theory and practice for empowerment and social justice* (3rd ed.). SAGE.

Meyer, B. (2015). *Sensational movies: Video, vision, and Christianity in Ghana*. University of California Press.

Mignolo, W., and Walsh, C. E. (2018). *On decoloniality: Concepts, analytics, praxis*. Duke University Press.

Mohammed, W. F. (2019). Journalistic griots: The marginalization of Indigenous language news and oral epistemologies in Ghana. *Radio Journal, 17*(2), 235–252.

———. (2021). Decolonizing African media studies. *Howard Journal of Communications, 32*(2), 123–138. https://doi.org/10.1080/10646175.2021.1871868

———. (2022a). Bilchiinsi philosophy: Decolonizing methodologies in media studies. *Review of Communication, 22*(1), 7–24. https://doi.org/10.1080/15358593.2021.2024870

———. (2022b). Dismantling the Western canon in media studies. *Communication Theory, 32*, 273–280. https://doi.org/10.1093/ct/qtac001

———. (2023a). Interrogating dominant ideology in media representations of witchcraft-related gendered violence: The case of Mariama Akua Denteh. *International Journal of Communication, 17*, 4778–4795.

———. (2023b). Intersectionality in African digital organizing: A Ghanaian perspective. *Communication, Culture & Critique, 16*(2), 107–109. https://doi.org/10.1093/ccc/tcad007

———. (2025). Afropolitanizing the local: how cultural imperialism is rewriting the narratives of African entertainment industries. *Cultural Studies*. https://doi.org/10.1080/09502386.2025.2469628

Motsaathebe, G., and Chiumbu, S. (Eds.). (2021). *Television in Africa in the digital age*. Palgrave Macmillan.

Moyo, L. (2020). *The decolonial turn: Towards a southern theory in media studies*. Springer.

Murray, S. (2014, September). The current state of scholarly journal publishing in Africa: Findings and analysis. *African Journals Online*. https://www.ajol.info/public/Scholarly-Journal-Publishing-in-Africa-Report-Final-v04c.pdf

National Communications Authority. (2023). *Authorised TV broadcasting stations*. Retrieved November 23, 2023, from https://nca.org.gh/television/

National Science and Maths Quiz. (2023, June 15). *How it all begun: The NSMQ story*. Retrieved June 22, 2024, from https://www.nsmq.com.gh/post/how-it-all-begun-the-nsmq-story

———. (n.d.). *Past winners: National champions*. Retrieved June 22, 2024, https://www.nsmq.com.gh/team-4

Ndlovu-Gatsheni, S. J. (2013). *Coloniality of power in postcolonial Africa: Myths of decolonization*. CODESRIA.

Ng, E., White, K. C., and Saha, A. (2020). #CommunicationSoWhite: Race and power in the academy and beyond. *Communication, Culture & Critique*, *13*(2), 143–151. https://doi.org/10.1093/ccc/tcaa011

Nkrumah, K. (1965, July 31). *Inauguration of Ghana television service*. Retrieved November 22, 2023, from https://ia802909.us.archive.org/30/items/inaugurationofghanatelevisionservice_20200416/InaugurationOfGhanaTelevisionService.pdf

NTV. (n.d.). Mission and Vision Statement. Tamale, Northern Region.

Nwulu, N. I., Adeyemi, A., Tochukwu, O., and Yemi, A. (2010). Television broadcasting in Africa: Pioneering milestones. In *2010 second region 8 IEEE conference on the history of communications*. IEEE. https://doi.org/10.1109/histelcon.2010.5735315

Olayiwola, A. (2011). Nollywood at the borders of history: Yoruba travelling theatre and video film development in Nigeria. *Journal of Pan African Studies*, *4*(5), 183–195.

Onuzulike, U. (2007). Nollywood: The birth of Nollywood: The Nigerian movie industry. *Black Camera*, *22*(1), 25–26.

———. (2009). Nollywood: Nigerian videofilms as a cultural and technological hybridity. *Intercultural Communication Studies*, *18*(1), 176–187.

Orjinmo, N. (2023, September 8). The Nigerians learning to speak with British accents. *BBC News*. www.bbc.com/news/world-africa-66569668

Ouattara, I. (2018). The griots of West Africa: Oral tradition and ancestral knowledge. In B. Reiter (Ed.), *Constructing the pluriverse: The geopolitics of knowledge* (pp. 151–167). Duke University Press.

Ouédraogo, A. (2007). The renewal of *Tales of the Lagle Naaba* on Burkina Faso's national television service. *Tydskrif Vir Letterkunde*, *44*(1), 155–167.

Park, M. J., and Curran, J. (2000). *De-Westernizing media studies*. Routledge.

Peltier, C. (2018). An application of two-eyed seeing: Indigenous research methods with participatory action research. *International Journal of Qualitative Methods*, *17*(1). https://doi.org/10.1177/1609406918812346

Prashad, V. (2022, June 20). Why Ghana allows US military base on its soil. *Mail & Guardian*. https://mg.co.za/thoughtleader/opinion/2022-06-20-why-ghana-allows-us-military-base-on-its-soil/

Roque, R. (2003). Equivocal connections: Fonseca Cardoso and the origins of Portuguese colonial anthropology. *Portuguese Studies, 19*(1), 80–109.

Rubin, H. J., and Rubin, I. S. (1995). *Qualitative interviewing: The art of hearing data.* SAGE.

Saboro, E. (2022). *Wounds of our past: Remembering captivity, enslavement and resistance in African oral narratives.* Brill.

Sagani TV. (n.d.). Mission and Vision Statement. Tamale, Northern Region.

Salawu, A. (2011). Essentials of Indigenous languages to journalism education in Nigeria. *Global Media Journal, 2*(1). https://doi.org/10.5789/2-1-31

Salih, M. A. (2021). Internal cultural imperialism: The case of the Kurds in Turkey. *International Communication Gazette, 83*(8), 733–752. https://doi.org/10.1177/1748048520928666

Schmidt, W. (2005). Mass media and visual communication: Popular posters in west Africa. *Third Text, 19*(3), 307–316. https://doi.org/10.1080/09528820500049296

Schudson, M. (1991). National news culture and the rise of the informational citizen. In A. Wolfe (Ed.), *America at century's end* (pp. 265–283). University of California Press.

Selasi, T. (2005, March 3). Bye-bye Babar. *LIP Magazine.* https://thelip.robertsharp.co.uk/2005/03/03/bye-bye-barbar/

Shohat, E., and Stam, R. (1994). *Unthinking Eurocentrism: Multiculturalism and the media.* Routledge.

Shome, R. (2000). Outing whiteness. *Critical Studies in Media Communication, 17*(3), 366–371. https://doi.org/10.1080/15295030009388402

———. (2019). Thinking culture and cultural studies—from/of the Global South. *Communication & Critical/Cultural Studies, 16*(3), 196–218. https://doi.org/10.1080/14791420.2019.1648841

Smith, K. B. (2010). Questions of source in African cinema: The heritage of the griot in Dani Kouyaté's films. *Journal of African Media Studies,* (2):1, 25–38.

Smith, L. T. (2012). *Decolonizing methodologies: Research and Indigenous peoples* (2nd ed.). Zed Books.

Smyth, R. (1979). The development of British colonial film policy, 1927–1939, with special reference to east and central Africa. *Journal of African History, 20*(3), 437–450. https://doi.org/10.1017/S0021853700017400

———. (2013). Grierson, the British documentary movement, and colonial cinema in British colonial Africa. *Film History, 25*(4), 82–113. https://doi.org/10.2979/filmhistory.25.4.82

Sobande, F. (2018). Black Feminist contributions to decolonising the curriculum. In J. Cupples & R. Grosfoguel (Eds.), Unsettling eurocentrism in the Westernised academy (pp. 87–99). Routledge.

Spivak, G. C. (1994). Can the subaltern speak? In P. Williams and L. Chrisman (Eds.), *Colonial discourse and post-colonial theory* (pp. 66–111). Routledge.

Stahl, R. (2010). *Militainment, Inc.: War, media, and popular culture.* Routledge.

Staniland, M. (1975). *The lions of Dagbon: Political change in Northern Ghana.* Cambridge University Press.

Steinhauer, E. (2002). Thoughts on an Indigenous research methodology. *Canadian Journal of Native Education, 26*(2), 69–81.

Stoller, P. (1992). *The cinematic griot: The ethnography of Jean Rouch.* University of Chicago Press.

Sulemana, T. (1970). *Naa Luro mini o bihi.* Bureau of Ghana Languages.

Tamale, S. (2020). *Decolonization and Afro-feminism*. Daraja Press.

Tomaselli, K. and Sakarombe, P. (2015). Griots, satirical columns, and the micropublic sphere. *Journal of African Media Studies, (7)*3, 315–27.

Townsend, L., and Lupin, D. (2021). Representation and epistemic violence. *International Journal of Philosophical Studies, 29*(4), 577–594. https://doi.org/10.1080/09672559.2021.1997398

Tricontinental: Institute for Social Research. (2018, October, 29). *Globalisation and its alternative: An interview with Samir Amin*. https://thetricontinental.org/globalisation-and-its-alternative/

Tsarwe, S. (2014). Voice, alienation and the struggle to be heard: A case study of community radio programming in South Africa. *Critical Arts, 28*(2), 287–310. https://doi.org/10.1080/02560046.2014.906345

Ugboajah, F. O. (1985). Oramedia in Africa. In F. O. Ugboajah (Ed.), *Mass communication, culture, and society in west Africa* (pp. 165–186). Hans Zell.

Ussher, Y. A. A., and Ollennu, Y. A. A. (2023). Promoting Ghanaian languages: The role of telenovela series. *Legon Journal of the Humanities, 34*(1), 92–117. https://doi.org/10.4314/ljh.v34i1.4s

van Staden, C. (2017). Watching Hong Kong martial arts film under apartheid. *Journal of African Cultural Studies, 29*(1), 46–62. https://doi.org/10.1080/13696815.2016.1236720

Virdi, J. (2017). A national cinema's transnational aspirations? Considerations on "Bollywood." *South Asian Popular Culture, 15*(1), 1–22. https://doi.org/10.1080/14746689.2017.1351785

Walker, C. A. (2009). Lest we forget: The Tuskegee Experiment. *Journal of Theory Construction & Testing, 13*(1), 5–6.

wa Thiong'o, N. (1986). *Decolonising the mind: The politics of language in African literature*. Heinemann.

———. (1993). *Moving the centre: The struggle for cultural freedoms*. J. Currey.

———. (2009). *Something torn and new: An African renaissance*. Basic Civitas Books.

———. (2012). *Globalectics: Theory and the politics of knowing*. Columbia University Press.

Willems, W. (2014). Provincializing hegemonic histories of media and communication studies: Toward a genealogy of epistemic resistance in Africa. *Communication Theory, 24*(4), 415–434.

Wolfe, E. H., III. (2001). *Extreme canvas: Hand-painted movie posters from Ghana*. Dilettante Press / Kesho Press.

Yamusah, M. S. (2013). *A critical study of the music industry in Tamale* [Master's thesis, University of Ghana]. UGSpace. https://ugspace.ug.edu.gh/handle/123456789/21614?show=full

Year of Return Ghana 2019. (n.d.). *About Year of Return*. Retrieved October 10, 2023, from https://www.yearofreturn.com/about/

Young, R. (2003). *Postcolonialism: A very short introduction*. Oxford University Press.

———. (2016). *Postcolonialism: An historical introduction*. John Wiley.

Zaa TV. (n.d.). Mission and Vision Statement. Tamale, Northern Region.

Filmography

Asadaachi (Iddris Abubakar Zimboo, 2004)
Baŋsim Chuɣu (Zaa TV, 2023)
Baɣa Kɔlgu (Alhassan Ali, 2007)
Dagbaŋ Salma Dundoŋ (Zaa TV, 2023)
Diabolo 3 (Bob Smith Jnr, 1992)
Duduhugu (NTV, 2017)
The Feminine Story (Sagani TV, 2023)
Gbewaa Bihi ni o Yaansi (Zaa TV, 2023)
Ghana's Most Beautiful (TV3, 2018)
Kavini (Sagani TV, 2023)
Kumkum Bhagya (Ekta Kapoor, 2014)
My Northern Achiever (Zaa TV, 2023)
Naabaala (Abdul Rahman Amangai, 1992)
Number 12 (Anas Aremeyaw Anas, 2018)
ŋuni Taali (Abubakari Sadiq, 1989)
Nuu ni Baŋsim (Sagani TV, 2023)
The Queen Classy Show (NTV, 2023)
Savannah (Kobi Rana, 2021)
Simpa Dance Competition (Zaa TV, 2023)
Tales of the Lagle Naaba (National Television of Burkina Faso, 2003)
Tamplima Saha (Zaa TV, 2023)
Touch of France (GHOne TV and Metro TV, 2019–2021)
Ya Nmaha (Alhaji Rashid Bawa BBC, 1990)
ʒemana Paɣaba (Zaa TV, 2023)

Index

About the Author

WUNPINI FATIMATA MOHAMMED was born and raised in Tamale, Ghana. She is an assistant professor in the Department of Communication at Cornell University. She is coeditor of *African Women in Digital Spaces: Redefining Social Movements on the Continent and in the Diaspora*.